Visualize Your Vocabulary

Turn Any SAT/ACT Word into a Picture and Remember It Forever

Volume 2

Shayne Gardner

To my wife Sheila—without your hard work and support, this VYV series would not be possible.

"When words fail, wars begin. When wars finally end, we settle our disputes with words." – Wilfred Funk

Copyright © 2016

Visualize Your Vocabulary: Turn Any SAT/ACT Word into a Picture and Remember It Forever, Volume 2

By Shayne Gardner

Illustrations: Kris Hagen

Editing: Sarah Wolbach

A portion of the proceeds from Visualize Your Vocabulary goes to:

Lost Dog & Cat Rescue Foundation

Mercury One

Marine Corps – Law Enforcement Foundation

Library of Congress Catalog Card Number:

ISBN-13: 978-1530346141

ISBN-10: 1530346142

Printed by CreateSpace

VisualizeYourVocabulary.com

Facebook.com/VisualizeYourVocabulary

Pinterest.com/SATwerdnerd

Twitter.com/SATwerdnerd

Google.com/+VisualizeYourVocabulary

VisualizeYourVocabulary@gmail.com

Table of Contents

Introduction

Why this book?

If you read *Visualize Your Vocabulary* and use this mnemonic aid for other SAT and ACT words not included here, you will gain a remarkable edge over students who do not. You will ingest the academic equivalent of steroids for an athlete.

The rationale for this book is simple. We think in pictures. Studies show most people are visual learners. The brain remembers pictures better than words. So if you want to learn new words as fast as possible, and actually enjoy the process, turn your words into pictures and skip the rote memorization.

Who should read this book?

Anyone who wants to expand their vocabulary should study this book. Moreover, because all of the 250 vocabulary words in *Visualize Your Vocabulary* are SAT and ACT words, the book is an invaluable resource for students preparing to take these or other standardized college entrance exams. It can also be extremely helpful for learning-disabled students, whether they are college-bound or not.

How it works

The simple trick of turning a word into a picture is called a mnemonic. We have used this memory technique from early childhood without knowing it. For example, we used pictures to learn the words to the nursery rhyme "Twinkle, Twinkle, Little Star." Mnemonics can be used to learn anything from algebraic formulas and history to grammar rules.

My favorite memory technique is converting the abstract definition of a word into a concrete "thing" that I can visualize in my mind's eye. Many times a difficult word I want to memorize doesn't want to stick. However, if I take the time to turn it into a picture, it sticks like Super Glue and I never forget it.

The trick is to come up with something familiar to you that rhymes with the word you want to learn. This rhyming word serves as the link, or bridge, between the word and the definition. I call this linking word the "memory word." Next, you turn the definition into a picture that includes the memory word. As an example, take the noun *alacrity*, which means "cheerful eagerness or readiness to respond; liveliness." My memory word is "a-black-kitty," a near perfect rhyme. My picture for *alacrity* is:

> Your **black kitty** is quite unusual. You return home after a long day at school and your six-foot-tall black kitty, who can walk on his hind legs, **cheerfully and eagerly** runs out to greet you. He does a few somersaults, grabs your backpack with a smile on his face, and carries it for you. Once inside the house, he pulls off your shoes, puts your slippers on your feet, cartwheels into the kitchen to pour your favorite drink, and lies down purring at your feet.

It's that simple. I used the rhyming word "a-black-kitty" to link the vocabulary word and the action picture that describes it. Now, whenever I hear or see the word *alacrity*, I think of what it sounds like, visualize the picture, and the definition comes flooding into my mind.

Rules of the game

A few simple rules make the picture stick like glue. If you don't use these rules when creating your own picture, you will certainly find it too boring and bland. Boring won't work, and you will forget the word.

Rule #1   Make the picture impossible, crazy, and illogical. In my picture for *alacrity*, the kitty is six feet tall, walks on his hind legs, carries a backpack, and does somersaults and cartwheels. Impossible! If the picture's scenario is possible or too logical, it will be difficult to remember the word. Crazy jumps out at you and is easily remembered.

Rule #2   Action! This is often incorporated with Rule #1, but it must be emphasized. The more movement and action you put into your picture, the more your mind's eye will notice it. This is similar to how we perceive movement with our peripheral vision. In my example for *alacrity*, "cheerfully and eagerly" is depicted with an abundance of action.

Rule #3   Personalize the picture in order to increase retention. If you insert yourself, a family member, or a close friend into the picture, you will be much more likely to remember it.

Rule #4   Exaggerate size and number. If an insect graces your picture, make it the size of a human, or even King Kong. A million insects might be better than just one. Remember, the kitty in *alacrity* is an abnormal size, standing six feet tall.

Rule #5   Use all five senses. If it stinks, make it reek so badly that you can feel your nose hairs curl up. If it smells good, make it euphoric. If you can hear it, amplify the sound. Taste it. Is it bitter, sweet, sour, or spicy? If it hits you, make it really hurt; maybe it gives you a bloody nose.

Rule #6   Add color. Who says that blood has to be red? That is too normal and logical. You will more easily remember the impossibility of blue or hot pink blood pouring out of your nose.

The common denominator for all of these rules is "nonsensical." Anything goes. The more impossible you make it, the better; the only limit is your imagination.

The format of this book

For each vocabulary word in the book, I provide the pronunciation, indicate its part of speech (noun, verb, etc.), define it, list several synonyms, and use it in a sentence. Some words can function as more than one part of speech. Many times, a word has multiple nuanced definitions; if so, I try to use the most common definitions. You will notice a theme with the sentences. If a sample sentence doesn't immediately come to mind as I am writing, I gleefully launch a salvo into the stereotypical politician's camp. I thoroughly enjoy goring that ox!

More than half of all English words stem from Latin, and many have Greek origins. If a word has a Latin origin, I point that out; if I find another origin interesting, I mention that as well. I have discovered that about 90 percent of SAT and ACT vocabulary words stem from Latin, and a few stem from Greek. Hence, my omission of most origins apart from these languages.

After all of the boring stuff, the fun begins. I provide the memory word and the action picture, followed by a snapshot illustration of the action picture, drawn by the wonderful artist Kris Hagen. On rare occasions, the illustration will look more generic than the written picture I created; I may need to do this to avoid copyright and trademark issues.

Use your creativity!

I strive to come up with a memory word that rhymes as closely as possible with the vocabulary word. I am not always completely satisfied with what comes to mind, but I do the best I can. You may come up with a better rhyming word and consequently a better picture. If so, use your own mnemonic instead of mine.

Have fun, and look for more volumes of *Visualize Your Vocabulary* in the near future.

Vocabulary Words

clairvoyant: (klair-**voi**-uhnt) **adjective** – perceiving things beyond the natural range of the senses; foreseeing the future

synonyms: extrasensory, intuitive, prescient, prophetic, psychic

origin: Comes to us through French, but ultimately from the Latin *clarus* and *videre*, meaning "to see clearly."

example: One with **clairvoyant** vision possesses a distinct advantage over those who depend only on their five senses.

memory word: clear-boy-ant

picture: When the ants want their palms read, want to speak to a deceased ancestor, or otherwise want to acquire information beyond what their five senses allow, they consult the oddly transparent *clear boy ant*, who possesses *extrasensory perception*.

subtle: (suht-l) **adjective** – difficult to detect or grasp by the mind; able to make fine distinctions

synonyms: faint, profound, refined, slight, suggestive, understated

origin: From the Latin *subtilis*, meaning "fine, thin, finely woven."

example: As their wedding anniversary neared, his wife's hints became less and less **subtle**.

memory word: shuttle

picture: The space *shuttle* leaves Earth's atmosphere on a mission to study the *faint* changes caused by weightlessness on living organisms. These *slight* changes require sensitive equipment for detection, since the human senses cannot perceive them. (NASA's Space Shuttle program lasted from 1981 to 2011; it comprised 135 missions.)

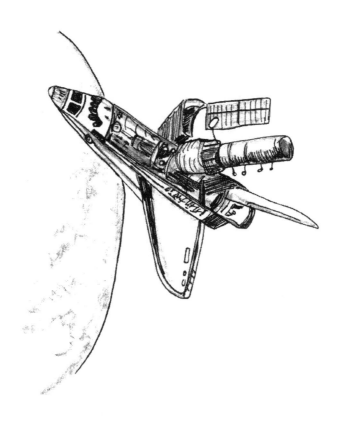

converge: (kuhn-**vurj**) **verb** – to come together from different directions; to end at a common result or conclusion

synonyms: assemble, come together, concur, join, merge, rally, unite

origin: From the Latin *convergere*, meaning "to incline together."

example: Almost 90,000 people **converged** on Dallas, Texas for the Restoring Love event on July 28, 2012.

memory word: con-merge

picture: Two convicts run at top speed, attempting a prison break. The *con*s will soon *merge* at a corner. This *con merge* will be very painful.

foible: (**foi**-buhl) **noun** – a minor weakness or failing of character; slight flaw or defect

synonyms: eccentricity, fault, idiosyncrasy, mannerism, quirk, vice

example: My parents have irritating oral **foibles**. After a meal, Dad loudly sucks air between his teeth in an attempt to clean them. Mom smacks her lips and says "aaahhh" after each sip of her coffee.

memory word: foil-ball

picture: Picture a friend you like everything about, except for one *minor flaw.* He carries a *foil ball* around with him, pretending to bounce it like a basketball and shooting it into wastebaskets. When he makes a basket, he shouts, "He shoots, he scores! The crowd goes wild!"

quandary: (**kwon**-duh-ree) **noun** – a state of perplexity or uncertainty, especially as to what to do in a certain situation

synonyms: dilemma, impasse, pickle, predicament, uncertainty

example: When two equally exceptional charter schools accepted Tommy, his parents found themselves in a **quandary.**

memory word: Juan-diary

picture: You share a dorm room with Juan and suspect he is a spy for the communist dictatorship of Cuba. Juan's diary lies on his desk, and he won't return for hours. You want to snoop to determine if he's a commie spy, but at the same time you don't want to violate his privacy. What to do in the *dilemma* of the *Juan diary?*

insipid: (in-**sip**-id) **adjective** – without distinctive, interesting, or stimulating qualities; without sufficient taste to be pleasing

synonyms: bland, dull, flat, tasteless, unappetizing, uninteresting, vapid

origin: From the Latin *insipidus,* meaning "tasteless."

example: I thought the evening would never end. I attended a networking party and sat between two boring people whose personalities were as **insipid** as the food on my plate.

memory word: N-sip-it

picture: A large N loudly sips *bland, lukewarm, and tasteless* juice. *N sip*s *it,* but doesn't enjoy it at all.

meticulous: (muh-**tik**-yuh-luhs) **adjective** – taking extreme care about minute details

synonyms: exact, fastidious, fussy, nitpicking, perfectionistic, precise

origin: From the Latin *meticulosus*, meaning "fearful, timid."

example: I don't know who is more **meticulous**, my brain surgeon or my accountant, but I'm glad of both.

memory word: Matt-tick-useless

picture: *Matt* the *tick* is *useless*. Since he *takes extreme care with the details*, it takes forever to get to the actual blood sucking. He has a thing with dog hair, so he shaves the target area, draws a target, applies sanitizer—and well, you get the point.

congregate: (**kong**-gri-gayt) **verb** – to come together, especially in large numbers

synonyms: assemble, convene, converge, gather, meet up, throng

origin: From the Latin *congregare,* meaning "to herd together, collect into a flock."

example: Wherever there is good beer, men will **congregate**.

memory word: Kong-Greg-gate

picture: Greg the football fanatic is best friends with King Kong. Wherever Greg goes, his buddy Kong follows. Every Sunday, Kong, Greg, and friends *gather together* for a tailgate party before the game. You might say they *Kong-Greg-gate*.

tenacious: (tuh-**nay**-shuhs) **adjective** – holding fast; keeping a firm hold

synonyms: determined, persevering, persistent, relentless, steadfast

origin: From the Latin *tenax*, meaning "holding fast, clinging."

example: Our legislators are **tenacious**; they want to raise our taxes, and by God, they will never give up.

memory word: tennis-shoes

picture: You take up rock climbing and buy a new pair of *tennis shoes* made specifically for the sport. They are called Mountain Claws because of the metal claws designed to dig into a surface and *keep a firm hold*.

arid: (ar-id) **adjective** – lacking sufficient water or rainfall; extremely dry

synonyms: barren, desert-like, dry as a bone, parched, waterless

origin: From the Latin *aridus*, meaning "dry, arid."

example: The big island of Hawaii has 11 of the world's 13 climate zones. One of these zones is **arid**.

memory word: air-it

picture: In the process of making the 13 climate zones of Earth, God decided to create Death Valley as one of the desert zones. He caused the wind to blow and blow to *air it* out and allowed *very little rainfall.*

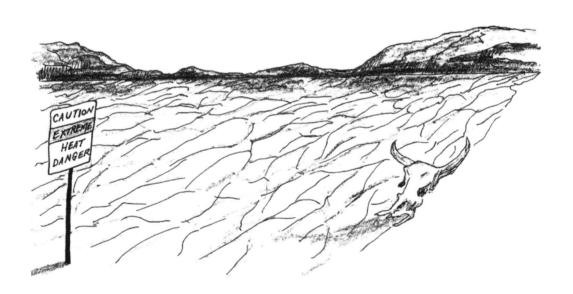

disdain: (dis-**dayn**) **noun** – lack of respect accompanied by a feeling of intense dislike; **verb** – to disrespect

synonyms: antipathy, aversion, contempt, derision; despise, hate

example: Some love the president, and others hold him in utter **disdain**.

memory word: dis-Dayne

picture: Poor Dayne gets no respect. People love to *dis Dayne*. They *despise* him and treat him with *contempt*.

compromise: (**kom**-pruh-mahyz) **noun** – an accommodation where both sides make concessions; **verb** – to expose or make liable to danger, suspicion, or disrepute

synonyms: agreement, deal, understanding, win-win; endanger, imperil

origin: From the Latin *compromittere*, meaning "to make a mutual promise."

example: Every successful relationship entails **compromises**.

memory word: compost-mice

picture: Mice invade your garden compost. You make a *deal* with them. You'll save some scraps just for them, if they'll stay out of your compost. The *compost mice* agree to this *arrangement*.

superficial: (soo-per-**fish**-uhl) **adjective** – being at, on, or near the surface; concerned with or comprehending only what is on the surface or obvious; not profound or thorough

synonyms: cursory, outward, perfunctory, shallow, skin-deep, surface

origin: From the Latin *superficialis*, meaning "pertaining to the surface."

example: With so much information and too little time, his lawyer could obtain only a **superficial** understanding of the case before the preliminary hearing.

memory word: super-fish-oil

picture: You massage some *super fish oil* into the eczema on your arm. It works great to soften the *surface* of the skin, but fails to treat the inflammation.

empathy: (**em**-puh-thee) **noun** – identification with and understanding of another's feelings

synonyms: compassion, concord, deep sympathy, insight

example: Women seem to have more intuition and **empathy** than most men.

memory word: M-Puffy

picture: The alphabet lines up alphabetically. The letter M, puffy and hurting, suffers from an allergic reaction to something. The letters L and N demonstrate their *compassion* in this way: The L bites its lip, saying, *"I feel your pain,"* and the N cries in *deep sympathy* while placing its arm around *M Puffy*.

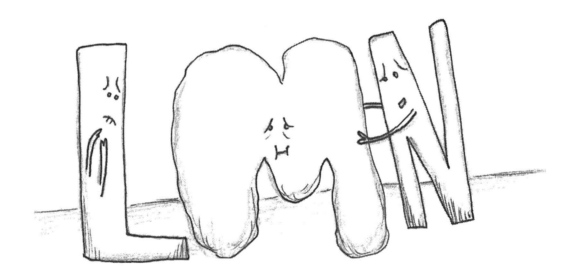

reconciliation: (rek-uhn-sil-ee-**ay**-shuhn) **noun** – the end of a disagreement and the renewal of a good relationship; the process of making it possible for two different ideas or facts to exist together without being opposed to each other

synonyms: accord, agreement, compromise, harmony, settlement

origin: From the Latin *reconcilare*, meaning "to make good again, restore, repair."

example: Will there ever be **reconciliation** between the Democrats and Republicans?

memory word: wreck-concentration

picture: In after-school study hall, there's an annoying and disruptive student who keeps *wreck*ing your *concentration*. After each interruption, you shoot a volley of spit wads at him. Finally, he calls for a truce and you *both agree to end the conflict*.

belie: (bih-**lahy**) **verb** – to show to be false; to misrepresent

synonyms: contradict, contravene, disprove

example: Burgeoning unemployment numbers **belie** the administration's claims that more Americans are finding work.

memory word: bee-lie

picture: You watch an animated version of *The Wizard of Oz*, called *The Wizard of Buzz*, in which all of the characters are bees. At the end of the movie, Dorothy and the gang discover the wizard is just an ordinary bee. They *disprove* the widespread belief in the great all-knowing Wizard of Buzz. Watch this movie and you'll see a *bee lie*.

conform: (kuhn-**fawrm**) **verb** – to behave and think in the same way as most other people in a group or society; to agree with or match something

synonyms: accommodate, adjust, comply, harmonize, obey, yield

origin: From the Latin *conformare,* meaning "to form, to shape."

example: I empathize with teenagers these days. The peer pressure to **conform** to a lower standard is hard to resist.

memory word: gun-form

picture: A young man thinks he's cool holding his gun sideways like a punk gangster. After a gun safety class, his *gun form* changes. He *adjusts* his form after studying the "wrong way" and "right way" pictures.

scrutinize: (**skroot**-n-ahyz) **verb** – to examine in detail with careful or critical attention

synonyms: analyze, dissect, inspect, investigate, peruse, study

origin: From the Latin *scrutari,* meaning "to examine, search."

example: Always thoroughly **scrutinize** any document before signing it.

memory word: screwed-in-nice

picture: The instructor at an auto mechanic school drifts around to each team of students as they learn how to use a torque wrench to tighten bolts perfectly. Using the torque wrench, he *carefully inspects* each bolt and observes, "Those are *screwed in nice* and tight."

assiduous: (uh-**sij**-oo-uhs) **adjective** – working very hard and taking great care that everything is done as well as possible; constant, unremitting

synonyms: attentive, diligent, exacting, indefatigable, scrupulous

origin: From the Latin *assidere*, meaning "to sit down to."

example: I recommend my handyman to everyone because of his **assiduous** work and attention to detail.

memory word: Sid-you-wuss

picture: The guys quit work to go out and grab a few drinks. One of them asks Sid if he's coming. He groans, "No, I need to finish my TPS report and bang out a few more details on this contract." His co-worker snorts, "***Sid, you wuss***. You're no fun. You're too ***diligent***."

emulate: (**em**-yuh-layt) **verb** – to attempt to equal or excel by imitation

synonyms: imitate, mimic, mirror, rival

origin: From the Latin *aemulari,* meaning "to rival, emulate."

example: It is important for children to strive to **emulate** their heroes.

memory word: emu-late

picture: All of the animals in the zoo participate in the *Imitate*-an-Ostrich contest. An emu shows up too late for the judging. Too bad the *emu*'s *late;* he would have *rivaled* all of the other contestants.

abstinence: (**ab**-stuh-nuhns) **noun** – the practice of not allowing yourself something (such as food, alcohol, or sex) for moral, religious, or health reasons

synonyms: asceticism, forbearance, self-denial, self-restraint

origin: From the Latin *abstinere,* meaning "to withhold, keep back."

example: Practicing **abstinence** requires self-control and will power.

memory word: abs-stance

picture: A guy with an awesome six pack *refrained from* all of his favorite foods to reveal his ripped abs. He hangs out at the beach every day so he can show off his abs. His abs look great, but must he hold that silly bodybuilder *abs stance?*

exemplary: (ig-**zem**-pluh-ree) **adjective** – worthy of imitation; being or serving as an illustration of a type

synonyms: commendable, excellent, ideal, laudable, meritorious, model

origin: From the Latin *exemplaris,* meaning "serving as a copy."

example: George Washington was a man of **exemplary** character.

memory word: except-Larry

picture: A teacher gushes to her class, "You have all been *model* students today. I *commend* you all—well, *except Larry*."

peccant: (pek-uhnt) **adjective** – guilty of a moral offense; violating a rule, principle, or established practice

synonyms: corrupt, erring, guilty, sinning

origin: From the Latin *peccare*, meaning "to make a mistake, to err or sin."

example: In a sane world, we would prosecute **peccant** politicians.

memory word: peck-it

picture: A religious woodpecker warns her children as they leave to play and explore for the day, "Don't bother Old Man Owl, who stands watch on the wooden cross in the church yard. Whatever you do, don't *peck it* or you'll be *guilty of sin!*"

surreptitious: (sur-uhp-**tish**-uhs) **adjective** – done secretly so no one will notice

synonyms: clandestine, covert, furtive, sneaky, stealthy, undercover

origin: From the Latin *surripere*, meaning "to seize secretly."

example: I was **surreptitious** in secretly planning a party for my wife.

memory word: syrup-dishes

picture: A family enjoys a Saturday night tradition of a "pancake breakfast" and a movie at home. There's always a big sticky mess to clean up on Sunday morning. One morning, the kids *surprise* Mom and Dad by rising early and *sneaking* downstairs to clean the *syrup*py *dishes*.

frugal: (**froo**-guhl) **adjective** – economical in use or expenditure; prudently saving or sparing; not wasteful

synonyms: meager, parsimonious, Spartan, stingy, thrifty, tight

origin: From the Latin *frugi*, meaning "useful, temperate, economical."

example: When the economy slows down, people have less money to spend and are forced to be **frugal**.

memory word: fruit-gull

picture: You love fruit. It's pretty much all you eat. You *hate to waste anything*, even the cores, stems, and seeds. Luckily, your pet sea gull eats all of the remaining fruit scraps. She's your *fruit gull*.

discredit: (dis-**kred**-it) **verb** – to injure the credit or reputation of; to show to be undeserving of trust or belief

synonyms: defame, disgrace, disparage, disprove, ruin, slander, smear

example: The myriad contradictions in the witness's testimony served to **discredit** him.

memory word: disc-read-it

picture: A double layer disc bragged that it could hold 8.5 gigabytes of data. Another disc demanded, "I don't believe it. Turn around so I can see your label." The first disc complied. After the second *disc read it*, it said, "Your label says you can hold only 4.7 gigabytes of data. I'm sorry to *disprove* your assertion, but you're wrong."

exasperate: (ig-**zas**-puh-rayt) **verb** – to irritate or provoke greatly

synonyms: aggravate, agitate, anger, rankle, rouse, vex

origin: From the Latin *exasperare,* meaning "to make rough, irritate, provoke."

example: I don't know which of my pet peeves **exasperates** me the most.

memory word: egg's-aspirin

picture: Eleven eggs in an open carton sing, "Ninety-nine bottles of beer on the wall." This *irritates* the twelfth egg to no end. They *aggravate* him so much that he resorts to taking aspirin for his headache. Hopefully, the *egg's aspirin* will kick in quickly.

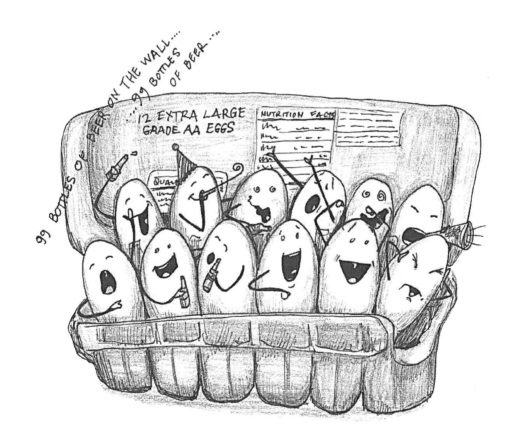

substantiate: (suhb-**stan**-shee-ayt) **verb** – to provide information or evidence to prove something is true

synonyms: confirm, corroborate, establish, support, validate, verify

origin: From the Latin *substantiare,* meaning "to give substance to."

example: Although I find no evidence to **substantiate** his existence, I still believe in Santa Claus.

memory word: sub-stands-she-ate

picture: A six-foot sub sandwich testifies in court. He accuses his wife of abusing him. The defense lawyer asks him, "Would you please show *proof* to *verify* this ridiculous claim?" The jury is horrified when the *sub stands* up, showing that *she ate* parts of him by taking huge bites.

prudent: (**prood**-nt) **adjective** – sensible and careful when making judgments and decisions; avoiding unnecessary risks

synonyms: circumspect, discerning, judicious, sagacious, shrewd, wise

origin: From the Latin *prudentem,* meaning "sagacious, circumspect."

example: If, during your annual medical check-up, your doctor says you have a rare disease that can only be cured with immediate brain surgery, it would be **prudent** to seek a second opinion.

memory word: student

picture: A young man, *wise and judicious* beyond his years, has studied the habits of highly effective people. He has been a good *student,* and now he too is *shrewd*.

obviate: (ob-vee-ayt) **verb** – to eliminate the need for something; to prevent something from happening

synonyms: avert, block, deter, forestall, interfere, preclude, ward off

origin: From the Latin *obvius*, meaning "that is in the way, that moves against."

example: It is only a matter of time before technology and competition **obviate** the need for the USPS.

memory word: Bob-V-8

picture: Bob hates veggies, but he eats the daily recommended serving because he knows it's good for him. Then he discovers V-8 juice. Now *Bob V-8* can drink his veggies, *making it unnecessary* for him to eat another veggie as long as he lives.

extenuating: (ik-**sten**-yoo-ay-ting) **adjective** – serving to make a fault, offense, illegal act, etc., appear less serious

synonyms: diminishing, downplaying, justifying, moderating, qualifying

origin: From the Latin *extenuare*, meaning "to lessen, reduce, diminish."

example: The judge's ruling was light due to **extenuating** circumstances.

memory word: extend-you-waiting

picture: You leave home in the morning for a job interview, allowing for the normal stop-and-go traffic, but a bad auto accident delays you, making you late for the interview. You explain this to the interviewer upon your arrival. Normally, tardiness would disqualify someone for a job interview, but the interviewer heard about the traffic jam and knew it would *extend you waiting* in traffic. He lets you reschedule the interview.

quell: (kwel) **verb** – to suppress or put an end to; to calm

synonyms: crush, extinguish, overcome, quench, stifle, stop, subdue

example: The riot police were called in to **quell** the furious protestors.

memory word: quail

picture: Every time Maude becomes anxious, angry, or stressed out, holding her pet *quail calms* her down. It *puts an end to* her crisis.

diligent: (dil-i-juhnt) **adjective** – quietly and steadily persevering, especially in detail or exactness; characterized by care and perseverance in carrying out tasks

synonyms: industrious, painstaking, persistent, steadfast, unrelenting

origin: From the Latin *diligentem,* meaning "attentive, assiduous."

example: My brother worked **diligently** with ancestry.com, tracing our family tree back to the *Mayflower*.

memory word: dill-against

picture: A dill pickle producer grows the best dill in the world. He gives *painstaking attention to every detail*, *carefully* planting, watering, cultivating, and harvesting the dill that makes his pickles the best. He brags, "I'll put my *dill against* all others and beat them every time."

submissive: (suhb-**mis**-iv) **adjective** – too willing to accept another person's authority and obey without questioning

synonyms: docile, malleable, meek, obsequious, pliable, yielding

origin: From the Latin *submittere,* meaning "to lower, reduce, yield."

example: The **submissive** Cold Mountain Penitentiary death row inmate marched the long green mile.

memory word: sub-missile

picture: A submarine threatens to fire a missile at another submarine. The sub *willingly submits*, throwing its hands up and pleading, "Don't shoot! I'll do whatever you want!" The *sub* with the *missile* crows, "Wow! That was easier than I expected."

demagogue: (**dem**-uh-gog) **noun** – a person, especially an orator or political leader, who gains power and popularity by arousing the emotions, passions, and prejudices of the people; **verb** – to treat or manipulate (a political issue) in the manner of a demagogue

synonyms: fomenter, inciter, instigator, politician, rabble rouser, radical

origin: From the Greek *demagogos,* meaning "popular leader, mob leader."

example: Adolf Hitler is one of history's most notorious **demagogues**.

memory word: den-of-dog

picture: You come home from school one day to discover your dog is a *radical rabble rouser*. You find him in the den delivering a rousing speech to a gathering of neighborhood dogs. He says to the *den of dog*s, "I'll say it again. You must rise up and chase every feline from the neighborhood, lest you wake up one day to find you are overrun with them."

provocative: (pruh-**vok**-uh-tiv) **adjective** – tending to provoke, excite, or stimulate

synonyms: incensing, inciting, spurring, stimulating

origin: From the Latin *provocativus,* meaning "calling forth."

example: Most of the White House press corps are lapdogs for the president, but one journalist asks probing and often **provocative** questions.

memory word: pro-chocolate

picture: A group of chocolate lovers meets every week in the mall at the Chocolate Crazy store to indulge their passion. A vanilla villain infiltrates the group's meeting, shouting, "Chocolate sucks! Death to chocolate! Down with brown! To hell with Hershey's! Viva la vanilla!" This *incites* the *pro chocolate* group to grab him, hold him down, and force-feed him some chocolate.

officious: (uh-**fish**-uhs) **adjective** – intrusive in a meddling or offensive manner

synonyms: dictatorial, interfering, opinionated, pushy, self-important

origin: From the Latin *officere,* meaning "to get in the way of."

example: After the residents of the retirement center reported the **officious** and bullying volunteer, he was asked to leave.

memory word: officials

picture: At halftime, the referees darted off the football field in a hurry. The teams entered their locker rooms a few minutes later to find the *intrusive officials* rifling through their lockers.

myriad: (**mir**-ee-uhd) **noun** – a large indefinite number; **adjective** – too numerous to count

synonyms: countless, infinite, innumerable, multitudinous

origin: From the Greek *myrias*, meaning "ten thousand, countless numbers."

example: The beach has **myriad** grains of sand, more than can possibly be counted.

memory word: Mary-and-Ed

picture: *Mary and Ed* were entered into *Ripley's Believe It Or Not* and *Guinness World Records* for having *a large number* of children that even *they couldn't count*.

collaborate: (kuh-**lab**-uh-rayt) **verb** – to work with others in order to produce or achieve something; to cooperate treasonably with an enemy

synonyms: collude, conspire, cooperate, join forces, team up, work with

origin: From the Latin *collaborare,* meaning "to work with."

example: The researchers **collaborated** to find a cure for the disease.

memory word: cold-lab-rat

picture: In a cage, several *cold lab rats work together* to build a fire to warm themselves. One twists a stick between his palms while another blows on the kindling. Several others block the view of the lab technicians so they can't see what the *cold lab rats* are up to.

garner: (**gahr**-ner) **verb** – to acquire or collect something, such as information, support, food, etc.

synonyms: amass, earn, gather, harvest, hoard, lay in, stockpile, store

origin: From the Latin *granarium,* meaning "a storehouse for grain."

example: The activist group **garnered** 100,000 signatures to put the measure on the ballot.

memory word: Carter

picture: President Jimmy *Carter,* our 39th president, was a wealthy peanut farmer before aspiring to become the leader of the free world. Imagine President *Carter gathering* a huge *stockpile* of enormous peanuts.

jaundiced: (**jawn**-dist) **adjective** – affected by or exhibiting envy, prejudice, or hostility; yellow or yellowish

synonyms: biased, bitter, cynical, prejudiced, resentful, skeptical

example: I base my **jaundiced** view of politicians on experience.

memory word: John-dust

picture: You live on the outskirts of town on a dirt road. John, your neighbor down the way, rides a *yellow* tractor past your house several times a day, stirring up dust. Even though he is a good neighbor, you *resent* him for the *John dust* he stirs up.

latent: (layt-nt) **adjective** – present but not visible or actualized; existing as potential

synonyms: dormant, inactive, inert, lurking, quiescent, sleeping, unseen

origin: From the Latin *latere,* meaning "to lie hidden."

example: Children have a large reserve of **latent** talent.

memory word: Latin

picture: You studied *Latin* for a couple of years in high school and became fairly proficient at it. However, life intervened; you went off to college, married, and started a family. Twenty years later, you find some time to take up *Latin* again and discover you didn't forget much. Your *Latin* just went *dormant*.

flagrant: (**flay**-gruhnt) **adjective** – openly and outrageously bad or shocking; showing no respect for people, laws, customs, etc.

synonyms: blatant, brazen, disgraceful, egregious, heinous, scandalous

origin: From the Latin legal term *flagrante delicto,* literally meaning "while the crime still burns," and figuratively referring to a criminal caught red-handed.

example: As a result of his **flagrant** disregard of traffic laws, he has a pile of unpaid speeding tickets.

memory word: fillet-grin

picture: You tie a vegetarian to a chair, determined to fillet a steak and make her eat it. An evil grin transforms your face while you fillet the steak. You call it your *fillet grin.* Now, that is **outrageously bad**!

loquacious: (loh-**kway**-shuhs) **adjective** – talking too much, often about trivial matters

synonyms: chatty, gabby, garrulous, motor mouth, talkative, verbose

origin: From the Latin *loquax*, meaning "talkative."

example: I met an interesting couple on our cruise. She was as **loquacious** as he was laconic.

memory word: low-places

picture: Garth Brooks follows you everywhere, telling you about all the people he knows in *low places.* He won't shut up about it. He keeps *talking nonstop.* If you are too young to know about Garth Brooks or have never heard his song *"Low Places,"* check it out online.

daunt: (dawnt) **verb** – to overcome with fear; to lessen the courage of

synonyms: cow, deter, discourage, intimidate, overawe, scare, shake

origin: From the Latin *domitare*, meaning "to tame, subdue."

example: The idea of going back to college to earn another degree and start a new career at age 50 is **daunting**.

memory word: dot

picture: A bully covered with red *dot*s threatens to touch you and give you the chicken pox. *Overcome with fear,* you run screaming from the building.

gravity: (grav-i-tee) **noun** – extreme importance or seriousness; the force of attraction by which terrestrial bodies tend to fall toward the center of the Earth

synonyms: concern, severity, significance, urgency

origin: From the Latin *gravitas,* meaning "dignity, seriousness."

example: She gave me a look of **gravity** that piqued my attention.

memory word: gravel-teeth

picture: While eating gravel, you chipped and broke several of your teeth. Your dentist is *very concerned* about your *gravel teeth*. He tells you, with a *serious* demeanor and voice, that there is *significant* damage.

digress: (dahy-**gres**) **verb** – to deviate or wander away from the main topic or purpose in speaking or writing

synonyms: drift, go off on a tangent, meander, ramble, roam, stray, veer

origin: From the Latin *digredi*, meaning "to go aside, depart, separate."

example: After the professor **digressed** for about five minutes, she finally found her way back to the topic and made her point.

memory word: high-grass

picture: You're hiking on a well-traveled path, but you *stray from* it, *veering off* into a field of **high grass**.

deplore: (dih-**plawr**) **verb** – to strongly disapprove of; to regret deeply

synonyms: abhor, bemoan, complain, criticize, denounce, lament

origin: From the Latin *deplorare,* meaning "to bewail, lament, weep bitterly."

example: Many parents **deplore** the state of the public school system.

memory word: deep-lure

picture: A man deep-sea fishes with his buddies. He *regrets* that they are not fishing for bass on a lake. He *complains*, "The lure must drop so deep, when a fish bites, it takes too much time and effort to reel in the *deep lure.*"

quisling: (**kwiz**-ling) **noun** – a person who betrays his or her country by aiding an enemy that has taken control of the country, often by serving in a puppet government

synonyms: Benedict, betrayer, collaborator, Judas, traitor, turncoat

origin: *Quisling* originated from a Norwegian pro-Nazi politician named Vidkun Quisling, who helped the Germans occupy Norway during World War II. He led the puppet government during the occupation and was tried for treason and executed at the end of the war. *Quisling* has become synonymous with *traitor* and *collaborator*.

example: The liberators swore that all **quislings** who had helped the enemy would be severely punished.

memory word: quiz-game

picture: One of the contestants on a popular *quiz game* show is an alien invader. Before the *quiz game* show begins, the host walks over to greet the alien. While shaking the hand protruding from the alien's forehead, he slips the quiz answers to him.

ebullient: (ih-**buhl**-yuhnt) **adjective** – overflowing with enthusiasm or excitement

synonyms: chipper, effervescent, elated, exhilarated, exuberant, vivacious

origin: From the Latin *ebullire,* meaning "to boil over."

example: If you just won the lottery, you would definitely feel **ebullient**.

memory word: a-bull-runt

picture: On a ranch with many cattle, *a bull runt* cartwheels, flips, and sings. He is very *excited, high-spirited, and vivacious*.

genial: (**jeen**-yuhl) **adjective** – warmly and pleasantly cheerful; a climate favorable for life, growth, or comfort

synonyms: amiable, blithe, convivial, friendly, kind, neighborly, pleasant

origin: From the Latin *genialis*, meaning "pleasant, festive."

example: Long after you graduate from high school, you will realize that your best teachers were **genial** but also tough and demanding.

memory word: Genie-Al

picture: Dozens of magic lamps wash up on the beach. Excited, you and other people rush down to the shore to snatch up the lamps. When the lamps are rubbed, genies pop out and immediately proceed with business, saying matter-of-factly, "Yes, master, you have three wishes. What is your first wish?" When *you* pick up a magic lamp and rub it, a ***pleasant, friendly*** genie pops out, gushing, "Hey there, how ya doing on this fine day? Nice day for a beach party. Nice to meet you. I'm ***Genie Al,*** the most ***amiable*** genie around. Would you care for some lemonade? A palapa, perhaps? These won't count toward your three wishes. Take your time, no rush."

frivolous: (**friv**-uh-luhs) **adjective** – not serious in attitude or behavior

synonyms: foolish, giddy, juvenile, playful, senseless, silly, whimsical

example: Want an example of a **frivolous** lawsuit? Christopher Roller sued famous magicians David Blaine and David Copperfield, insisting they reveal the secrets of their magic tricks to him. He also demanded a portion of their income for life. He claimed he was God and they were infringing on his powers, using them to perform tricks. I'm being serious, not **frivolous.** This is a true story!

memory word: free-balloons

picture: Exasperated parents attend the Ban Carnivals Convention. They don't want any more carnivals in their town. Creepy-looking carneys show up at the convention and skip around handing out *free balloons* and engaging in *playful and silly* antics.

deprecate: (**dep**-ri-kayt) **verb** – to express strong disapproval of; to depreciate or belittle

synonyms: derogate, detract, disparage, pooh-pooh, put down, run down

origin: From the Latin *deprecari*, meaning "to entreat against."

example: Seniors often **deprecate** freshmen by dissing them and making them feel unimportant.

memory word: Debra-cake

picture: At Grandpa's birthday party, *Debra* ate the whole *cake* by herself. Now she's covered with cake and icing, and everyone at the party *frowns with disapproval*.

ineffable: (in-**ef**-uh-buhl) **adjective** – incapable of being expressed or described in words; not to be spoken because of its sacredness

synonyms: indefinable, indescribable, inexpressible

origin: From the Latin *ineffabilis,* meaning "unutterable."

example: While saying her vows, the bride struggled to express her **ineffable** feelings in words. Her tears of joy expressed her feelings quite well.

memory word: an-elfin-bull

picture: Last night you had a strange, incoherent dream. During breakfast with your family, you attempt to describe the dream, in which **an elfin bull** did **indescribable** things. Unfortunately, you **can't find the words** to explain its antics.

grandiloquent: (gran-**dil**-uh-kwuhnt) **adjective** – using long or complicated words to impress people

synonyms: aureate, bombastic, dramatic, magniloquent, pompous

origin: From the Latin *grandiloquus*, a combination of *grandis* (big) + *loquus* (to speak), meaning "to speak big, lofty speech; bombastic."

example: The senator gave one of his typical **grandiloquent** speeches, impressing no one but himself.

memory word: grand-elephant

picture: The circus is in town! The world's largest *grand elephant* flies over the audience, *pompously* reciting poems with *impressive-sounding words*.

verbose: (ver-**bohs**) **adjective** – using more words than are needed

synonyms: loquacious, prolix, talkative, voluble, windy

origin: From the Latin *verbosus,* meaning "full of words."

example: Many of the bills signed into law are too **verbose** and complicated—by design, of course.

memory word: Herb-hosts

picture: Herb is a people person. *Herb hosts* a party and *talks nonstop* from the arrival of his first guest to the departure of the very last at 1 a.m. At 1:01 a.m., he calls a friend and talks to him for several hours.

inert: (in-**urt**) **adjective** – unable to move or resist motion

synonyms: immobile, inactive, languid, phlegmatic, sluggish, torpid

origin: From the Latin *inertis*, meaning "unskilled, inactive, slothful."

example: After Thanksgiving dinner, most of us feel bloated and **inert** for the remainder of the day.

memory word: N-hurt

picture: A big letter N is in a full body cast due to a serious injury. The *N hurt*s, and the cast renders it *immobile*.

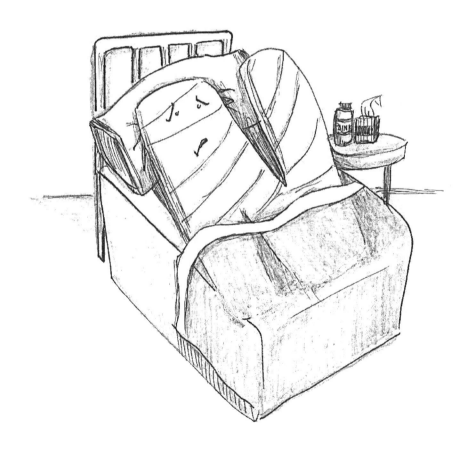

xenophobia: (zee-nuh-**foh**-bee-uh) **noun** – an unreasonable fear or hatred of foreigners or strangers or of something foreign or strange

synonyms: narrow-mindedness, parochialism, prejudice

example: Harry and Sally make an odd couple. One is **xenophobic** and the other likes to travel around the world and study other cultures.

memory word: zebraphobia

picture: A rancher buys a zebra at a horse auction. He brings the zebra home and puts him in the corral with several horses. The horses, *afraid of this odd-looking foreigner*, cower in fear in the corner of the corral because of their *zebraphobia*.

homage: (**hom**-ij) **noun** – something said or done to show respect for a person or thing

synonyms: adulation, deference, honor, loyalty, obeisance, tribute

example: When we say the Pledge of Allegiance, we pay **homage** by removing our hats and placing our right hands over our hearts.

memory word: huh-Madge?

picture: A couple grew up listening to the hair bands of the 70s and 80s. They attend an Atomic Punks (Van Halen *tribute* band) concert. A *tribute* band loves a particular band so much that they *honor* them by only playing the music of their idols. On the way home, Madge asks her husband what he thought about the concert. His ears ringing from the loud music, he asks, *"Huh, Madge?"*

acquiesce: (ak-wee-**es**) **verb** – to comply silently or without protest

synonyms: accede, accept, agree, cave in, consent, give in, yield

origin: From the Latin *acquiescere,* meaning "to rest."

example: In this sense, "to rest" means to become passive in the face of something you oppose, causing you to **acquiesce.**

memory word: crack-the-S

picture: A letter S sits in a chair in a dark interrogation room. One light bulb hanging overhead shines in its eyes. After enduring an hour of torture, it finally *gives in* and *agrees* to divulge the information its interrogators want. When they successfully *crack the S,* it sobs, "Okay, Okay—I'll talk!"

irresolute: (ih-**rez**-uh-loot) **adjective** – not able to decide what to do

synonyms: hesitant, indecisive, tentative, uncertain, unsure, wavering

example: The **irresolute** child stood with her face pressed against the glass, unable to decide which flavor of ice cream she wanted. Meanwhile, the line behind her grew longer by the minute.

memory word: eerie-salute

picture: You join a secret club when you go off to college. After they swear you in as a member, they show you the secret handshake and salute. The handshake is harmless enough, but the *eerie salute* resembles the Nazi salute a little too much. Suddenly, you're *not so sure* you want any part of this club.

redolent: (**red**-l-uhnt) **adjective** – having a strong, pleasant odor; making you think of the thing mentioned (usually used with "of" or "with")

synonyms: evocative, fragrant, remindful, reminiscent, scented

origin: From the Latin *redolere,* meaning "to emit a scent, diffuse odor."

example: Once in a while, I detect a whiff of a woman's perfume **redolent** of the perfume my first girlfriend wore.

memory word: red-uh-lint

picture: On Mother's Day, your dad takes over Mom's chores. Before he starts the laundry she tells him, "Make sure you check all the pockets." A couple of hours later she calls him into the laundry room. Holding up the lint filter in one hand and an empty tube of cherry-flavored lip balm in the other, she snaps, "What's this?" He sheepishly mutters, ***Red...uh...lint?*** I guess I forgot to check the pockets, huh?" Now all of our clothes have the ***strong fragrance*** of cherry. This will ***remind*** her of his kind gesture whenever she wears those clothes.

pernicious: (per-**nish**-uhs) **adjective** – having a very harmful effect on somebody or something, especially in a way that is gradual and not easily noticed

synonyms: baleful, damaging, deadly, destructive, harmful, nefarious

origin: From the Latin *pernicies,* meaning "destruction, disaster, ruin."

example: If you've seen *The Cable Guy*, starring Jim Carrey, you know how **pernicious** too much TV can be.

memory word: fur-fishes

picture: Furry fish in your huge aquarium beat up the other fish and tear up the scenery. The *exceedingly destructive fur fishes* even manage to break the glass. You come home to find your carpet soaked with 100 gallons of water and several dead fish.

dubious: (**doo**-bee-uhs) **adjective** – causing doubt; unsettled in mind; of doubtful quality

synonyms: dubitable, iffy, questionable, skeptical, suspicious, uncertain

origin: From the Latin *dubiosus,* meaning "doubtful, uncertain."

example: If you are **dubious** about the benefit of learning another language, don't be. Although challenging, it will be rewarding.

memory word: doobie-bus

picture: Doobie smoke billows out the windows of a bus loaded with hippies. They entice you to go along on the *doobie bus* for a road trip. You are *uncertain* about this. A little devil pops up on your left shoulder and tells you to climb aboard and enjoy yourself. As you step onto the bus, a little angel appears on your right shoulder advising, "Just say no." Although you are *skeptical*, you follow the angel's advice and step off the bus.

jeopardize: (jep-er-dahyz) **verb** – to risk harming or destroying something or somebody

synonyms: endanger, hazard, imperil, risk, stake

example: People who post questionable pictures of themselves on Facebook **jeopardize** losing their jobs.

memory word: leper-dice

picture: A disfigured, leprous hand appears out of nowhere and drops a pair of dice into your hand. Fear overcomes you as you realize the *leper dice,* contaminated by a deadly disease, *endanger* you and may *destroy* your health.

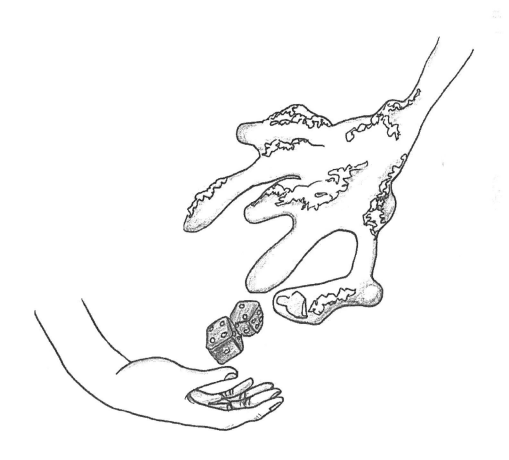

apocryphal: (uh-**pok**-ruh-fuhl) **adjective** – of doubtful authorship or authenticity

synonyms: counterfeit, dubious, fake, questionable, spurious

origin: From the Greek *apokryphos*, meaning "hidden, obscure."

example: Not long after the new kid transferred to my school, **apocryphal** stories about his past started circulating.

memory word: a-pocket-full

picture: You stroll into a pawn shop with *a pocket full* of *fake* diamonds, hoping to pass them off as authentic. The owner examines them closely and looks at you with a skeptical eye. He is very *doubtful of the authenticity* of these *fake* diamonds.

gesticulate: (je-**stik**-yuh-layt) **verb** – to move your hands and arms about in order to attract attention or make somebody understand what you are saying

synonyms: gesture, motion, pantomime, signal, wave

origin: From the Latin *gesticulus*, meaning "to mimic."

example: I couldn't help but wonder what the transient was thinking as he **gesticulated** wildly and talked to himself.

memory word: just-stick-in-lake

picture: You stand on the shore of a lake *gesturing and motioning* frantically to everyone to come look at something. You think it's a snake, but upon closer examination you realize it is *just* a *stick in* the *lake*.

insidious: (in-**sid**-ee-uhs) **adjective** – intended to entrap or beguile; stealthily treacherous or deceitful; working or spreading in a hidden and usually injurious way

synonyms: cunning, ensnaring, guileful, menacing, perfidious

origin: From the Latin *insidiosus*, meaning "cunning, treacherous."

example: The **insidious** effect of the mainstream media is evident in the polls and at the ballot box.

memory word: in-city-rust

picture: The Oxidizer, a *cunning and treacherous* villain, releases a gas that quickly oxidizes everything it comes in contact with—except for gold and silver. Metal, brick, and even glass rust. Food rots before it can be eaten. He changes the name of the city to City Rust. While the mayor, police, and of course the local superhero endeavor to figure out what is going on and how to catch this *perfidious* perp, The Oxidizer busies himself *in City Rust* stealing everyone's gold and silver.

rudimentary: (roo-duh-**men**-tuh-ree) **adjective** – being in the earliest stages of development; being or involving basic facts or principles

synonyms: elementary, embryonic, primitive, undeveloped, vestigial

origin: From the Latin *rudimentum*, meaning "early training, first experience."

example: As you can tell, I am fascinated by the Latin origins of many English words. However, my grasp of Latin is **rudimentary** at best.

memory word: rude-mint-tree

picture: There's a mint tree in an *elementary* school yard. The children want to get close to the mint candies dangling from its limbs, but the *rude mint tree* makes them cry by saying things like, "I've had it up to my limbs with short kids"; "Hey, dog breath, if I throw a stick, will you go away?"; and "If idiots and uncoordinated children were trees, this place would be an orchard."

beset: (bih-**set**) **verb** – to attack on all sides; to surround or hem in; to annoy continually; to decorate or cover lavishly (as with gems)

synonyms: assail, besiege, encircle, encompass, harry, infest, invade

example: His football team is **beset** with injuries and unlawful behavior among the key players.

memory word: bees-sit

picture: You enter an empty subway car and find a place to sit down. At the next stop, a gang of bees embark and crowd around you. The *bees sit* right next to you. They *surround* you and *annoy* you.

sententious: (sen-**ten**-shuhs) **adjective** – trying to sound important or intelligent through the use of big words, especially by expressing moral judgments; concise and full of meaning

synonyms: aphoristic, expressive, pithy, pointed, terse, to the point

example: The politician's speech abounded in aphorisms and moralizing. Everyone left convinced that he was just a **sententious** blowhard.

memory word: send-dentures

picture: Three generations live in the same house. On Grandma and Grandpa's anniversary, the family treats them to their favorite restaurant down the street. Thirty minutes after they leave, you receive a text saying, "*Send dentures*. Can't masticate meticulously (chew carefully)." Grandpa is always *terse and concise;* he likes to use big, *pretentious* words.

inchoate: (in-**koh**-it) **adjective** – not yet completed or fully developed; just begun; not organized; lacking order

synonyms: embryonic, formless, inceptive, nascent, shapeless, unfinished

origin: From the Latin *incohare,* meaning "to begin."

example: Her **inchoate** idea quickly developed, ultimately leading to her winning entry in the National Science Fair.

memory word: ink-coat-it

picture: You open a tattoo shop called *Ink Coat It*. Although you are open for business, everything in the shop is *unfinished and disorganized.* Good luck!

certitude: (**sur**-ti-tood) **noun** – state of being certain; free from doubt

synonyms: assuredness, certainty, confidence, conviction, sureness

origin: From the Latin *certitudo,* meaning "that which is certain."

example: "They make the best burgers. You're going to love this diner," she said with **certitude**.

memory word: certain-dude

picture: The Loch Ness Monster emerges from the end of a wave tube on a surfboard for a brief moment, before it dives underwater. A surfer excitedly exclaims, "Whoa! Dude! I just saw a sea monster surfing. Did you see that?" The other surfer retorts, "No, man. You *sure?*" The first surfer confirms, "I'm *certain, dude.*"

intrinsic: (in-**trin**-sik) **adjective** – belonging to or part of the real nature of something or somebody

synonyms: built in, congenital, elemental, inborn, inherent, innate

origin: From the Latin *intrinsecus*, meaning "inwardly, on the inside."

example: Many teachers do what they do for the **intrinsic** reward of helping children learn.

memory word: a-train-set

picture: Little girls *inherently* imagine themselves princesses and play with dolls. What do little boys *congenitally* want, besides taking things apart so they can see what is inside and playing cowboys and Indians? That's right, they want *a train set*. A little boy's *built in* desire is to be a train conductor.

laud: (lawd) **verb** – to praise, glorify, or honor

synonyms: acclaim, adore, eulogize, extol, revere, venerate, worship

origin: Laudanum is a drug consisting of alcohol and opium. Its creator knew that the people who ingested this concoction loved the way it made them feel. He named it after *laudere,* the Latin word for "to praise."

example: Laudanum was one of the world's most **lauded** drugs for over 350 years. The inventor's name, you ask? Philippus Aureolus Theophrastus Bombastus von Hohenheim; you can call him by his nickname, Paracelsus.

memory word: God

picture: You float in the clouds, *lauding God* and *singing his praises*.

endemic: (en-**dem**-ik) **adjective** – native to or confined to a certain region; originating where it is found

synonyms: local, regional

origin: From the Greek *endemos*, meaning "native, belonging to a people."

example: Yellow Fever was **endemic** to Panama at the turn of the 20th century, when the U.S. built the Panama Canal. Thankfully, Dr. Gorgas' theory that mosquitoes caused Yellow Fever was the first step to the disease's eradication.

memory word: end-of-Mick

picture: Mick took a vacation in Los Angeles. Why? We'll never know. Mick walked down the street and unwittingly crossed a boundary into an area controlled by a *local* gang. The "*natives*" don't approve of just anyone entering without permission. Unfortunately, that was the *end of Mick*.

tyranny: (**tir**-uh-nee) **noun** – unfair or cruel use of power or authority; the rule of a tyrant; a country under this rule

synonyms: despotism, dictatorship, fascism, oppression, totalitarianism

example: Any political system that does not allow dissent is a **tyranny**.

memory word: tear-on-knee

picture: A tyrant rules *with absolute and cruel power*. Anyone coming into his presence must kneel when they enter the room and approach him on their knees. Those who report to him often, have blisters and scabs on their knees. Every time they are summoned, they add another *tear on knee*. Then they are punished for leaving blood on the floor.

marred: (mahrd) **adjective** – damaged or spoiled so as to render less perfect, attractive, or useful; disfigured, defaced, or scarred

synonyms: blemished, dinged, stained, sullied, tainted, tarnished

example: The awesome game was **marred** by the rioting fans.

memory word: Maude

picture: *Maude,* the crazy cat lady, has *scars, scratches, and blemishes* from handling all of her cats.

sardonic: (sahr-**don**-ik) **adjective** – scornfully or cynically mocking

synonyms: biting, caustic, mocking, mordant, sarcastic, satirical

origin: From the Greek *sardonios,* meaning "scornful laughter."

example: The sketch writers for late night comedy talk shows use a lot of **sardonic** humor.

memory word: he's-hard-on-it

picture: At a comedy club, a lion tells one *sarcastic* joke after another about the laughing hyena sitting on a stool next to him. Mr. Lion quips, "I'm thinking of giving up weed, because it's making me paranoid. Although it doesn't help that my girlfriend has Tourette's and owns this pet hyena." Ba dum tshh. Mr. Lion *mocks* the poor hyena relentlessly. You might say *he's hard on it.*

fervor: (fer-ver) **noun** – great warmth or very strong feeling

synonyms: ardor, earnestness, enthusiasm, intensity, passion, zeal

origin: From the Latin *fervor*, meaning "boiling heat, seething foam."

example: Patrick Henry delivered his "Give Me Liberty or Give Me Death" speech with great patriotic **fervor**.

memory word: fur-boar

picture: A boar with a ***strong passion*** for furs wears his favorite fox fur. The other boars find him a little odd and refer to him as the ***fur boar***.

pivotal: (**piv**-uh-tl) **adjective** – of vital or crucial importance

synonyms: cardinal, central, critical, essential, focal, momentous, vital

example: Graduation from high school and college are **pivotal** events in one's life.

memory word: divot-tool

picture: You work at the most eminent golf resort in the world. All of the other employees look up to you with high esteem because you hold the most *important and central position*. You use the golden *divot tool* to replace the golfers' divots.

impugn: (im-**pyoon**) **verb** – to criticize; to challenge someone or something as false or wrong; to cast doubt upon

synonyms: contradict, disaffirm, dispute, negate, oppose, question

origin: From the Latin *pugnare,* meaning "to fight." Related derivatives *pugilist* and *pugnacious* also refer to combativeness and fighting.

example: The candidate **impugned** his opponent's character by suggesting that he is dishonest.

memory word: imp-you

picture: You studiously plow through the SAT exam. While you attempt to determine which vocabulary word best fits the context of a passage, an imp appears and *questions* your choice, *casting doubt* in your mind. The superhero Werdnerd appears and bellows, *"Imp! You* scram or I'll throw the book at you!"

lionize: (**lahy**-uh-nahyz) **verb** – to treat someone as a famous or important person

synonyms: acclaim, adulate, exalt, glorify, honor, idolize, praise

example: Savannah's classmates **lionized** her when she earned a perfect score on the SAT.

memory word: lion-eyes

picture: A world-renowned lion tamer possesses a strange ability to peer into the eyes of a lion and mesmerize it, compelling it to act according to his desire. He's training some amateur lion tamers who *idolize* him. He demonstrates his abilities by looking into the *lion's eyes*, compelling the lion to jump up on a pedestal. The other tamers *oohh!* and *aahh!* in *exaltation.*

obligatory: (uh-**blig**-uh-tohr-ee) **adjective** – required due to moral or legal obligation

synonyms: binding, compulsory, mandatory, necessary, requisite

example: It amuses me how often we respond to the greeting "How's it going?" with the **obligatory** "How's it going?" Rather than answer the question, we repeat the question. Even more amusing is when someone asks the **obligatory** "How's it going?" and we respond with "Not much" because we were anticipating, "What's going on?" Or is it just me?

memory word: old-pig-tore-it

picture: Two honorable farmers share a boundary as neighbors. If either farmer's animals do any kind of harm or damage to the other farmer's animals or property, they feel *morally required* to make amends for the transgression. One farmer's 700 lb. old pig tore down part of the fence separating their farms and trampled the other's garden. The farmer insists, "Well, my *old pig tore it* down and ruined your garden so I'm *bound* to fix that fence and give you what you deem is fair from my garden."

lethargic: (luh-**thahr**-jik) **adjective** – lacking the energy or enthusiasm to accomplish a task

synonyms: enervated, languid, languorous, slothful, sluggish, torpid

example: There's something about Thanksgiving dinner that makes most of us feel **lethargic**.

memory word: leopard-chick

picture: The freshly hatched chicks look normal, except for one oddball. She has leopard spots and is *sluggish and enervated*. The *leopard chick* sleeps on and off all day while the other chicks follow Mom around.

unerring: (uhn-**er**-ing) **adjective** – undeviatingly accurate; not liable to error or flaw

synonyms: certain, exact, faultless, impeccable, infallible, perfect

example: Katniss, **unerring** with a bow and arrow, never misses her target.

memory word: nun-earring

picture: The nuns at St. Mary's Catholic School participate in a fun spelling bee contest. The nun with the ABC earrings wins the spelling bee because she makes it to the end *without making a mistake*. She is known thereafter as *Nun Earrings*.

futile: (**fyoot**-l) **adjective** – incapable of producing the desired result

synonyms: hopeless, impractical, ineffective, in vain, pointless, useless

origin: From the Latin *futilis,* meaning "vain, worthless."

example: Your ambition to learn challenging vocabulary will not be **futile** if you study this book carefully.

memory word: flute-oil

picture: A slick door-to-door salesman just sold you a 55-gallon barrel of *flute oil*. You don't even own a flute, and you can't think of any practical use for it. It is *useless* to you.

pejorative: (pi-**jawr**-uh-tiv) **adjective** – having a disparaging, derogatory, or belittling effect; making something seem less valuable or worthwhile

synonyms: critical, derisive, rude, slighting, uncomplimentary

origin: From the Latin *pejorare,* meaning "to make worse."

example: **Pejorative** is the opposite of euphemistic. If you call a tree-hugger an environmentalist, you are using a euphemism. If you call an environmentalist a tree-hugger, you are using a **pejorative** term.

memory word: jar-give

picture: Twin girls receive a dozen roses each from their dates. One date presents his roses in a crystal vase. The other presents his in a crusty old jar. The jar makes the roses *seem less valuable and worthwhile*. The *jar give*s an *uncomplimentary* message to the second girl.

castigate: (**kas**-ti-gayt) **verb** – to criticize or reprimand severely

synonyms: berate, censure, chasten, chastise, excoriate, rebuke, upbraid

origin: From the Latin *castigare,* meaning "to correct, reprove, chastise."

example: As Junior pulled into the driveway, he braced himself because he knew his dad would **castigate** him for denting the family car.

memory word: cast-break

picture: The cast on your shoulder and arm proves hard to adjust to. You can't seem to maneuver without knocking something over with your cast. Your mom, exasperated by your breaking things with your cast, *criticizes* your destructiveness and sends you to your room for a *cast break*.

orthodox: (**awr**-thuh-doks) **adjective** – conforming to what is commonly accepted; whether it be a religion, ideology, doctrine, belief, attitude, behavior, etc.

synonyms: conservative, conventional, customary, sanctioned, traditional

origin: Latin borrowed *orthodoxus* from Greek's *orthodoxos*, meaning "having the right opinion."

example: An **orthodox** person is not likely to say or do anything radical.

memory word: or-throw-rocks

picture: You travel way back in time, taking *conventional* weapons with you for protection. You bump into a caveman who challenges you to a duel. You can use your gun or your knife . . . *or throw rocks*.

blasphemy: (**blas**-fuh-mee) **noun** – behavior or language that insults or shows a lack of respect for God, religion, or anything considered sacred

synonyms: desecration, heresy, impiety, irreverence, profanity, sacrilege

origin: Latin borrowed *"blasphemia,"* meaning "a speaking ill, impious speech, slander," from Greek.

example: Taxation is sacred to both conservatives and liberals. It would be a **blasphemy** for a conservative to vote to raise taxes, and it would be blasphemous for a liberal to vote to cut taxes.

memory word: blast-for-me

picture: A militant atheist burns a cross and a Bible on your front lawn. Ranting and raving, he shouts, "I hate your God! It's a *blast for me* to be *irreverent to your God!*"

malinger: (muh-**ling**-ger) **verb** – to pretend to be ill, usually in order to avoid work

synonyms: dodge, evade, fake, loaf, sham, shirk

example: Kids sometimes **malinger** to avoid school or work. Adults rarely malinger because their work piles up and threatens to bury them.

memory word: my-finger

picture: The finger you broke two months ago has already healed and feels fine, but you milk it by *pretending* it still needs the brace, thereby *avoiding* your chores at home. The friends who type your assignments for your classes must continue for a while longer. When you ask someone for a favor, you hold up your hand and groan, *"My finger."*

expunge: (ik-**spuhnj**) **verb** – to strike out, wipe out, or otherwise erase something

synonyms: abolish, annihilate, annul, cancel, delete, efface, eradicate

origin: From the Latin *expungere,* meaning "to blot out, mark for deletion."

example: The principal promises to **expunge** all of the offenses from my record for the entire year if I pledge to be on my best behavior until graduation.

memory word: X-sponge

picture: A wet, X-shaped sponge scoots down the sidewalk, unaware that it is *erasing* the kids' chalk drawings. *X-sponge* asks, "Hey kids, what cha doin'? Hey, why you lookin' at me like you wanna squeeze me dry?"

tenuous: (ten-yoo-uhs) **adjective** – thin or slender in form; lacking substance or significance; lacking in clarity

synonyms: delicate, fine, flimsy, light, narrow, questionable, shaky

origin: From the Latin *tenuis,* meaning "thin."

example: The **tenuous** threads of a spider's web break easily.

memory word: tin-U.S.

picture: Your geography teacher assigns a project for students to build a model of the United States. You are allowed to build it out of any material you desire, and you choose tin foil. You manage to transport your model to class without any damage, but within minutes, someone crushes your *thin and flimsy tin U.S*. Fortunately, you took pictures of it so your teacher can see what it looked like.

lament: (luh-**ment**) **verb** – to feel or express grief, sorrow, or regret

synonyms: bemoan, bewail, deplore, mourn, rue, sob, wail, weep

origin: From the Latin *lamentari,* meaning "wailing, weeping."

example: The nation **lamented** the passing of George Washington.

memory word: la-mint

picture: Your prize-winning French poodle choked to death on a mint candy. Naturally, you *express great sorrow* for her passing, *mourning* that your little Frenchie was done in by *la mint*.

adulterate: (uh-**duhl**-tuh-rayt) **verb** – to corrupt, debase, or make impure by adding inferior materials, ingredients, or elements

synonyms: cheapen, contaminate, defile, denature, devalue, pollute, taint

origin: From the Latin *adulterare,* meaning "to falsify, corrupt."

example: Santa didn't want to **adulterate** the perfect layer of fresh snow on all the rooftops, but he had a job to do.

memory word: adult-grapes

picture: Imagine some *adult*s making wine by crushing *grapes* the old-fashioned way, with their feet. Unfortunately, one of them has a severe case of athlete's foot, which *contaminates* the grapes.

obfuscate: (**ob**-fuh-skayt) **verb** – to make something obscure or unclear, usually deliberately; to confuse or bewilder; to make less distinct, or darken

synonyms: cloud, conceal, confound, dim, fog, muddle, perplex

origin: From the Latin *obfuscare,* meaning "to darken."

example: Politicians **obfuscate** their positions on issues to confuse voters and win elections.

memory word: off-you-skate

picture: You propel yourself to the moon using a giant slingshot. After landing on the moon, *off you skate* to its *dark and indistinct* side.

sage: (sayj) **noun** – a wise person who is venerated for his or her wisdom, judgment, and experience; a plant belonging to the genus *Salvia*, used in medicine and cooking

synonyms: discerning, enlightened, insightful, judicious, sagacious

origin: From the Latin *sapere,* meaning "to discern, be wise."

example: The Chinese **sage** sat under a tree and meditated.

memory word: sage

picture: A witch doctor says that if you eat *sage* it will make you very *wise*. So you scarf down a bushel of *sage* and poof!, you turn into a *wise* old owl.

fatuous: (**fach**-oo-uhs) **adjective** – lacking intelligence

synonyms: asinine, dense, idiotic, inane, mindless, puerile, vacuous

origin: From the Latin *fatuus*, meaning "foolish, insipid, silly."

example: Her beauty drives her admirers to **fatuous** demonstrations of affection.

memory word: fat-you-was

picture: You bump into a *really dumb* guy who hasn't seen you since you lost 100 pounds. He notes, "I don't understand what my eyes is tellin' me. *Fat you was*, but thin you is now. Is you playin' a goof on me with smoke and mirrors, like what they have in the carnival my cousin works at?"

mordant: (**mawr**-dnt) **adjective** – sharply biting or sarcastic in speaking or writing; **noun** – an acid or other corrosive substance

synonyms: acerbic, biting, cutting, cynical, pointed, sardonic, sharp

origin: From the Latin *mordere,* meaning "to bite, nip, sting."

example: The students enjoyed the professor's **mordant** wit.

memory word: board-ant

picture: An old and somewhat eccentric ant sits on a bench in front of the Five & Dime store on Main Street. The children hang around because they are fascinated and entertained by the *sharp wit* and *pointed* antics of the *"board ant,"* as they call him. When someone walks by, he makes a *sarcastic* remark about them and takes a *bite* out of a board he holds in his hand. He chews it like tobacco while he waits for the next person to walk by. When he spits it out, the kids *oohh* and *aahh* as the *caustic* expectorant burns a hole in the sidewalk.

craven: (kray-vuhn) **adjective** – lacking courage; contemptibly timid

synonyms: cowardly, fearful, gutless, poltroon, scared, timorous, yellow

example: The Cowardly Lion discovered that, in the end, he was not so **craven** after all.

memory word: raven or haven

picture: When Howard opens his front door, a seven-foot-tall *raven* stands motionless, peering menacingly at him. Howard slams the door shut and *gutlessly* runs to the safe *haven* of his basement. The *raven* squawks, "Howard's a *coward*! Howard's a *coward*!"

irascible: (ih-**ras**-uh-buhl) **adjective** – easily provoked to anger

synonyms: cantankerous, cranky, irritable, petulant, querulous, testy

origin: From the Latin *irasci,* meaning "to be angry, be in a rage."

example: The **irascible** old codger down the street always yells at the neighborhood kids, "Get off my lawn!"

memory word: harass-a-bull

picture: A bullfighter waves his red flag, thumbs his nose, teases, and otherwise harasses the bull. The bull, *growing angrier* by the minute, stirs up dust with his front hooves while steam barrels out of his nose and ears. Only the best bullfighters dare *harass a bull*.

sapid: (**sap**-id) **adjective** – having taste or flavor; agreeable as to the mind; to one's liking

synonyms: appealing, attractive, engaging, palatable, savory, zestful

origin: From the Latin *sapere*, meaning "to taste, have good taste."

example: Because I love hot food, a dish must contain a lot of spice to have a **sapid** quality.

memory word: zap-it

picture: Your magic taser gun comes in handy when a particular meal isn't **appealing** to you. After you **zap it** with your taser, it suddenly becomes **palatable**.

caustic: (kaw-stik) **adjective** – capable of burning, corroding, or destroying living tissue; severely critical or sarcastic

synonyms: acerbic, acid, acrid, biting, erosive, mordant, pungent

origin: From the Latin *causticus*, meaning "burning, acrid."

example: The corporation's CEO delivered a **caustic** speech to rebut the senator's slam on "Big Business."

memory word: caw-stick

picture: A crow wanders around saying, "Caw, Caw," while poking other crows with its *caw stick*. *Acid* oozes from the stick, *burning* the crows. Once the crow has their attention, it *severely criticizes* their flaws.

impudent: (**im**-pyuh-duhnt) **adjective** – showing a lack of respect for others; improperly forward or bold

synonyms: audacious, brazen, cocky, insolent, presumptuous

origin: From the Latin *impudens*, meaning "brazen, insolent, shameless."

example: The student remained in detention after school for the rest of the week for his **impudent** behavior.

memory word: imp-you-dent

picture: As you study in the library, an *insolent* imp appears and distracts you. You warn him to go away and let you focus, but he continues to *behave disrespectfully*. You throw a book and hit him in the head so hard it leaves a dent. The *imp you dent* should have listened.

malediction: (mal-i-**dik**-shuhn) **noun** – a slanderous accusation; calling down a curse which usually serves as an insult

synonyms: curse, execration, expletive, imprecation, jinx

origin: From the Latin *maledictare,* meaning "to curse, abuse, slander."

example: Joan hurt her sister's feelings with the **malediction** "Go jump in a lake."

memory word: Mao-addiction

picture: The communist dictator Mao exhibits a strange addiction. Several times a day, he gets his fix by *cursing or insulting* another person. If he doesn't satisfy this urge to *denunciate* someone, he suffers from profuse sweating and the shakes. He feels better immediately after satisfying his *Mao addiction.*

sophistry: (**sof**-uh-stree) **noun** – the use of clever arguments to persuade someone that something is true when it is really false

synonyms: ambiguity, deception, fallacy, inconsistency, trickery

origin: From the Greek *sophos*, meaning "wise, clever."

example: The argument that giving children contraceptives reduces teen pregnancy and disease is pure **sophistry**. This only encourages promiscuous activity. Abstinence education actually does reduce both teen pregnancy and disease.

memory word: sofa-street

picture: A man and his worn-out *sofa* are out on the *street*. His wife kicked him out of the house, and he's trying to convince her with a *clever argument* that he will change his ways. With fingers crossed behind his back, he explains how he will change if she will only take him back.

fulsome: (fuhl-suhm) **adjective** – excessively generous in praise, thanks, or apologies to the extent that you sound insincere

synonyms: flattering, ingratiating, sycophantic, unctuous

example: Hollywood stars seem to line up to give **fulsome** praise to communist dictators; one of their favorites is Fidel Castro.

memory word: fool-some

picture: A politician just finished giving another campaign speech chock full of lies. His *sycophantic* aide *compliments him endlessly* with *nauseating flattery*. He gushes, "As they say, you can *fool some* of the people all of the time and all of the people some of the time, but you, sir, can fool all of the people all of the time."

rapacious: (ruh-**pay**-shuhs) **adjective** – excessively greedy; devouring food in huge amounts; subsisting by the capture of living prey

synonyms: avaricious, marauding, predatory, ravenous, voracious

origin: From the Latin *rapere,* meaning "to seize."

example: Third-world dictators are **rapacious**. Some receive millions in foreign aid from the United States, intended to help their people. However, most of the money lands in their personal bank accounts. Thus, they live a life of luxury while their people live in poverty.

memory word: Rap-Aces

picture: Unfortunately, there's a new rap group whose CD reached platinum status. They rap about *preying on people and taking their stuff*. They call themselves the *Rap Aces*.

languorous: (**lang**-ger-uhs) **adjective** – characterized by a lack of energy, vitality, spirit, liveliness, or interest

synonyms: apathetic, enervated, languishing, lazy, phlegmatic, sluggish

origin: From the Latin *languere,* meaning "to be weary, faint, listless."

example: When you wake up early but decide to stay in bed for another hour or two, you can enjoy the feeling of doing absolutely nothing as you luxuriate in **languorous** bliss.

memory word: lane-guru

picture: Murphy's Law dictates that whichever lane of rush hour traffic you change to becomes the most *sluggish* lane. A driving instructor called the *Lane Guru* has a knack for picking the least *inert* lane for his students in rush hour traffic.

prevaricate: (pri-**var**-i-kayt) **verb** – to be deliberately ambiguous or unclear; to mislead or create a false impression

synonyms: dodge, equivocate, evade, falsify, misrepresent, tergiversate

origin: From the Latin *praevaricare*, meaning "to transgress, sin against, violate."

example: In Job 1:7 and Job 2:2, Satan **prevaricates** when God asks him from where he is coming, saying, "From going to and fro on the earth, and from walking back and forth on it."

memory word: pretty-berry-cake

picture: Little Werdnerd's mom can't determine if he is owning up to sneaking a slice of the ***pretty berry cake*** she just finished decorating, or if he is denying it. He uses big words to ***deliberately mislead*** his mom. He snickers, "Although a child of my age is highly prone to committing terminological inexactitudes, I assure you that I am neither ***equivocating*** nor ***tergiversating*** as to the verity of the locality of the absent confection."

choleric: (kol-er-ik) **adjective** – easily angered; extremely irritable

synonyms: irascible, peevish, quick-tempered, testy, touchy, wrathful

example: It's amazing how a nap can transform a **choleric** person into a pleasant, easy-going teddy bear.

memory word: color-it

picture: An OCD child colors in her coloring book. Her crayons are all laid out perfectly in a rainbow pattern. When she colors out of the lines ever so slightly, she throws her crayon across the room in a *fit of wrath*. She says, "I can't *color it* right!"

enigma: (uh-**nig**-muh) **noun** – a person, thing, or occurrence that is puzzling and difficult to understand

synonyms: bewilderment, conundrum, mystery, parable, riddle

origin: From the Latin *aenigma,* meaning "riddle."

example: Mystery surrounds the Bermuda Triangle. Many have reported the **enigma** of disappearing planes and ships, UFO sightings, time warps, freak waves, and other phenomena within its boundaries.

memory word: an-egg-mon

picture: A Jamaican walks up to you and says, "From a distance I thought you had a halo over your head, but now I can plainly see it is *an egg, mon.* I *do not understand*. I am *bewildered,* mon."

abstruse: (ab-**stroos**) **adjective** – difficult to understand

synonyms: enigmatic, esoteric, incomprehensible, perplexing, recondite

origin: From the Latin *abstrusus,* meaning "hidden, concealed, secret."

example: Algebra comes easily to some; to others it could not be more **abstruse**.

memory word: abs-to-roots

picture: A dude complains to his doctor, "I just ***don't understand*** it. One day I have ripped abs, and the next day some roots are growing out of them!" ***Abs to roots*** is ***hard to understand.***

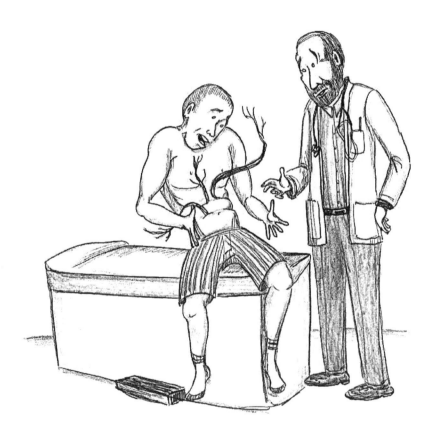

torpid: (**tawr**-pid) **adjective** – inactive or sluggish; hibernating or in suspended animation

synonyms: apathetic, dormant, inert, languid, motionless, paralyzed

origin: From the Latin *torpere*, meaning "to be numb or stiff."

example: If you don't want to become **torpid** in old age, you must stay active both mentally and physically.

memory word: tar-pit

picture: A Velociraptor is mired in a *tar pit*. It is usually very fast, but it has been in the *tar pit* so long that it is *lethargic and sluggish*.

brazen: (bray-zuhn) **adjective** – something done openly, without shame, that people find shocking; made of brass

synonyms: audacious, brash, impertinent, insolent, unabashed

example: She broke up with her boyfriend on Thursday and was **brazen** enough to be seen kissing and holding hands with his best friend on Friday.

memory word: raisin

picture: A bunch of raisins are doing their job — lying out in the sun, drying out. Except for the brazen *raisin,* that is. He's decked out in shades, under a parasol, and slathering on sunscreen, sipping a cool, refreshing coconut drink. How *audacious!*

vainglorious: (vayn-**glawr**-ee-uhs) **adjective** – exhibiting vanity or pride in one's own abilities or achievements; feeling self-important

synonyms: arrogant, boasting, conceited, egotistic, haughty, pompous

example: Insufferable and **vainglorious**, she constantly brags about all of her beauty contest trophies.

memory word: fang-glorious

picture: A *vain* vampire thinks he's all that. Unlike all other vampires, this "vainpire" can see himself in a mirror and stops at every one to check out his marvelous fangs. He looks at himself and gushes, "You are one gorgeous sucker. Those *fang*s are *glorious*."

bellicose: (**bel**-i-kohs) **adjective** – exhibiting an eagerness to fight; aggressively hostile

synonyms: antagonistic, combative, pugnacious, quarrelsome, warlike

origin: From the Latin *bellicosus,* meaning "warlike, valorous."

example: The **bellicose** thug infiltrated the peaceful protest, bloodied a few noses, and even bit off someone's finger.

memory word: bell-on-coast

picture: The Liberty ***Bell on*** the ***coast*** is ***hostile*** and ***looking for a fight***. It shakes its fist at a surfer on his way out to catch some waves and yells, "Yeah, that's right. Keep on walkin' or I'll ring your bell."

contumacious: (kon-too-**may**-shuhs) **adjective** – stubbornly resistant to authority

synonyms: contrary, froward, insubordinate, obdurate, recalcitrant

origin: From the Latin *contumax*, meaning "insolent, obstinate."

example: Mules are **contumacious**, but "contumacious as a mule" doesn't have the same ring to it as "stubborn as a mule."

memory word: con-tomato-juice

picture: The warden summons a convict to his office and tells him he can't keep threatening to beat up other convicts for not giving him their tomato juice at mealtime. He insists, "You've done this so many times they call you *'con tomato juice.'* If you continue to ***stubbornly resist my authority***, it's solitary confinement – AND no more tomato juice for you!"

heed: (heed) **verb** – to pay close attention to

synonyms: caution, consider, listen up, mark, mind, note, notice, regard

example: If the United States of America would **heed** the lessons of history, we would not be in such a mess.

memory word: feed

picture: You babysit a humongous baby. The mom gives you strict instructions to *pay attention to* the clock. She says, "You must *feed* Junior every hour on the hour. You will *notice* that he becomes very grumpy when he goes more than an hour without eating."

vexation: (vek-**say**-shuhn) **noun** – something or someone causing anxiety or annoyance

synonyms: aggravation, agitation, hassle, irritation

origin: From the Latin *vexare*, meaning "to distress, afflict, irritate."

example: The stresses of the day piled up until she finally collapsed and wept in **vexation**.

memory word: next-station

picture: Driving cross-country, a man stops at a gas station in the middle of nowhere, only to discover that it is out of gas. Driving on, he sees a sign indicating that the ***next station*** is 100 miles down the road. ***Annoyed and irritated***, he pounds on the steering wheel, causing the airbag to deploy.

foppish: (fop-ish) **adjective** – excessively refined and vain in taste and manner, usually used to describe a man

synonyms: dandified, dapper, elegant, fashionable, natty

example: His manner of dress, speech, and gesturing all scream **foppish**.

memory word: crawfish

picture: A *dapper* gentleman visits some friends in Louisiana. They say, "Hey, let's fix up a mess of *crawfish* tonight." He responds, "Thank you, no. I wouldn't partake of that lowly crustacean if you put a gun to my head. A fine lobster and sushi would better suit my *refined taste*."

petulant: (**pech**-uh-luhnt) **adjective** – easily irritated or annoyed, especially if you can't do or get what you want

synonyms: grouchy, huffy, impatient, querulous, testy, whiny

origin: From the Latin *petere,* meaning "to attack, assail."

example: The honor roll student acted like a **petulant** child when he received a B minus on his science project.

memory word: pet-you-lent

picture: Your huge St. Bernard, Bernie, only eats and sleeps. Your neighbor borrows him to use as a pack animal on a week-long backpacking excursion. *Huffy* and *irritable*, your neighbor returns Bernie a week later. He throws the leash at you, saying, "I spent $50 on food for this worthless *pet you lent* me. I expected him to carry some of my gear, but he refused, so I had to carry a 100-pound pack! Thanks for nothing, jerk!"

cloister: (kloi-ster) **noun** – a covered walkway with arches around a courtyard, usually as part of a convent or monastery; **verb** – to seclude oneself from the world, as in retirement or for religious studies

synonyms: sanctuary; confine, isolate, retreat, sequester

origin: From the Latin *claudere,* meaning "to shut, make inaccessible."

example: Once again, Spitwad Sam is **cloistered** in the classroom during recess while his classmates play outside.

memory word: toy-store

picture: A grown man in a ***toy store*** plays with a train set similar to the one he enjoyed as a kid. As a little boy, he dreamed of being a train conductor. Today, he relives memories of playing with his train set for hours on end. He's in his own little world, ***secluded from the world*** around him. The toy store employee attempts to draw him out of his reverie to inform him the store closed ten minutes ago.

protract: (proh-**trakt**) **verb** – to draw out or lengthen in time or space

synonyms: defer, delay, drag out, prolong, stall, stretch out

origin: From the Latin *protrahere,* meaning "to draw forth, prolong."

example: Experts foresee **protracted** negotiations between the Senate Democrats and Republicans to end the budget impasse and avoid a government shutdown.

memory word: Pro-Track

picture: A dad takes his kids to the ***Pro Track*** Go-Kart raceway. They arrive to discover it closed because they are *extending the length and width* of the track to accommodate bigger and faster go-karts.

puerile: (**pyoo**-er-il) **adjective** – displaying or suggesting a lack of maturity; childishly foolish or immature

synonyms: adolescent, infantile, jejune, juvenile, silly

origin: From the Latin *puerilis*, meaning "childish." *Puerilis* comes from *puer*, meaning "boy."

example: Female humor is much more mature than the **puerile** humor some men enjoy.

memory word: pure-oil

picture: Mom comes home from grocery shopping, puts away the groceries needing refrigeration, then instructs the kids to sit and watch TV for a few minutes while she lies down to rest. Ten minutes later, she finds that the *silly, immature*, and messy kids have dumped a container of pure olive oil on the kitchen floor and are playing in it. It's not *pure oil* anymore.

ambiguous: (am-**big**-yoo-uhs) **adjective** – having several possible meanings or interpretations; difficult to understand

synonyms: indefinite, muddy, obscure, questionable, unclear, vague

origin: From the Latin *ambigere,* meaning "to dispute about."

example: Even highly trained CPAs find many parts of the 75,000 page federal tax code **ambiguous** at best.

memory word: amphibious

picture: A zebra notices a creature resembling a lizard crawl out of a pond. The zebra says, "Now, what might you be? You resemble a lizard, but you live in the water, so you must be a fish." The creature retorts, "I'm *amphibious*. I live on land and in water." The zebra says, "I'm *unclear* what you mean. I *can interpret that several ways*. You are a fish resembling a lizard; therefore, you should jump back in the water or you'll soon die. Or, you are a lizard and you were taking a swim, which means that you're pulling my leg."

bovine: (**boh**-vahyn) **adjective** – dull and slow-moving like a cow

synonyms: inert, slow-witted, sluggish, stolid

origin: From the Latin *bos*, meaning "ox, cow."

example: The mob boss's bodyguard may be **bovine** physically and mentally, but he is inhumanly strong and can handle a gun, too.

memory word: bow-vine

picture: A cow falls into a deep ravine and can't extract herself. Some of her friends lower a vine. They tie a pretty bow and a message onto the vine reading, "Grab on. We'll pull you up!" However, the cow is too *dull* to figure out what they want her to do. Even though she has been given a *bow vine* with an invitation, she is too *slow-witted* to follow the instructions.

oblique: (oh-**bleek**) **adjective** – done or stated in an indirect manner; slanting at an angle

synonyms: angled, askew, diagonal, inclined, indirect, sideways

origin: From the Latin *obliquus,* meaning "slanting."

example: Most muscles are named according to their location, origin and insertion, shape, size, function, or layout of muscle fibers. For example, the internal and external **obliques** run at an angle to the midline of the body.

memory word: O-blink

picture: Imagine an O whose blinks last for a couple of seconds. The O also has an inner ear problem, which causes it to lose balance when it blinks. The *O blink*s and leans *sideways at an angle.*

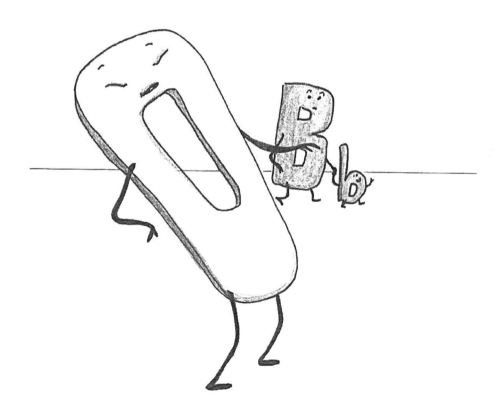

jejune: (ji-**joon**) **adjective** – without interest or significance; having a lack of maturity; deficient or lacking in nutritive value

synonyms: dull, empty, inane; childish, immature, juvenile, puerile

origin: From the Latin *jejunus,* meaning "fasting, empty, meager."

example: She made **jejune** remarks about the play, demonstrating that she didn't understand its complexity.

memory word: Juh-June

picture: You and your friends relax at the coffee shop, discussing which month is the *least interesting*. It's Stuttering Sam's turn to opine, and he sputters, "*Juh-June* is the least suh-significant month because you have to go to a bunch of *dull* wuh-weddings and stuff."

insubordinate: (in-suh-**bawr**-dn-it) **adjective** – the refusal to obey the orders of an authority figure

synonyms: contumacious, defiant, intractable, mutinous, recalcitrant

example: The soldier was court-marshaled for constant **insubordination**.

memory word: in-sub-order-knit

picture: You stop in the middle of preparing a sub sandwich for a customer and sit down to knit a sweater. The manager snaps, "I've had enough! The next time you quit *in sub order* to *knit,* you're fired!"

troglodyte: (**trog**-luh-dahyt) **noun** – one who lives in a cave; someone living in seclusion; a person out of touch with world affairs

synonyms: caveman, primitive; hermit, recluse

origin: From the Greek *troglodytes*, meaning "cave-dweller; one who creeps into holes."

example: We are raising a nation of **troglodytes** who spend most of their time playing video games, unaware what's happening in the real world.

memory word: frog-you-bite

picture: Believe it or not, there's an urban myth called "frog licking." The myth holds that a particular frog in southern Arizona, when licked, secretes a hallucinogenic compound. The secretion is a poison that can kill you. No such frog exists, so don't go looking for it. However, for this entry of *Visualize Your Vocabulary*, let's pretend it does. Imagine some prehistoric stoners (pun intended) licking frogs to catch a buzz. One *caveman* bites his frog and the other knuckle dragger scolds, "No Zug! Frog you lick, NOT *frog you bite*."

hubris: (**hyoo**-bris) **noun** – excessive pride

synonyms: loftiness, overbearing, pomposity, self-importance, vanity

origin: From the Greek *hybris*, meaning "insolence, outrage."

example: Filled with **hubris**, the candidate gave an impassioned speech, boasting that he can solve the nation's problems because he is a genius.

memory word: Hugh-Briss

picture: Huey Brisscole, a Renaissance man, can repair anything. He's an accomplished artist, plays several instruments (is classically trained), and speaks several languages fluently. He is *full of pride* and *overly self-confident*. He has no friends, due to his insufferable demeanor. His acquaintances call him *Hugh Briss*; the name rhymes with *hubris* and describes him perfectly.

lugubrious: (loo-**goo**-bree-uhs) **adjective** – mournful or gloomy, especially in an affected or exaggerated manner

synonyms: blue, depressive, melancholy, pensive, sad, somber, sorrowful

origin: From the Latin *lugere,* meaning "to mourn."

example: A funeral dirge is a **lugubrious** tune expressing emotions of mourning and grief.

memory word: lagoon-virus

picture: Natives paddle a canoe into the lagoon of a nearby island. The scouts disembark and walk onto the beach. Seconds later, they collapse because they have inhaled a fast-acting *lagoon virus.* Those still in the canoe become *exaggeratedly mournful* at the sudden passing of their scouts.

odious: (**oh**-dee-uhs) **adjective** – deserving or causing hatred; very offensive

synonyms: abhorrent, abominable, detestable, loathsome, repugnant, vile

origin: From the Latin *odiosus,* meaning "hateful, offensive."

example: The **odious** senator frequently makes offensive comments about his constituents.

memory word: oh-yes

picture: The *Fear Factor* contestants must eat a plate of *repugnant* blood clots and mealworms in less than two minutes. The host, Joe Rogan, asks the first contestant if he is ready and he gushes, "*Oh yes!*" One of the other contestants quavers, "I *hate* you and this *detestable* game!"

slough: (sluhf) **verb** – to shed, cast off, or get rid of

synonyms: discard, drop, shake off, throw away

example: Rattlesnakes **slough** off their skin every year; this cast-off skin is often in one piece.

memory word: stuff

picture: A hoarder owns way too much *stuff*. She hires the organizing guru Peter Walsh to help sift through it all, *discard* the junk, and catalogue what remains. His mantra is, "*Shed* the clutter, clear the mind!"

incessant: (in-**ses**-uhnt) **adjective** – continuing without interruption

synonyms: ceaseless, constant, endless, everlasting, nonstop, relentless

origin: From the Latin *incessans,* meaning "unceasing."

example: On the flight, I was surrounded by the **incessant** and cacophonous sounds of coughing, crying babies, and nonstop talking by the guy sitting next to me.

memory word: ant-says-ant

picture: Question: What does an ant say when you ask it what it is, over and over again?

Answer: The *ant says "ant," continuously*.

Corny, yes, but I bet you will remember what **incessant** means!

nurture: (**nur**-cher) verb – to provide care, support, and encouragement; to train or educate

synonyms: bring up, foster, nourish, parent, raise, rear, sustain

origin: From the Latin *nutrire,* meaning "to suckle."

example: He secretly **nurtured** a dream to be a professional athlete.

memory word: nerd-chair

picture: A super brainiac at your school is so intelligent that she finds the advanced honors classes boring. Therefore, the school provides her with a special room. Her computer station is equipped with several oversized monitors. She sits in a top-of-the-line ergonomic chair with a built-in back massager, heater, and cooler—all voice-activated. They call it the ***nerd chair***. Every 15 minutes, a teacher checks in to ***provide nourishing snacks and encouragement***.

ascetic: (uh-**set**-ik) **adjective** – leading an austere and simple life of self-denial, and rejection of comforts and luxuries; **noun** – a person who lives this way

synonyms: abstemious, abstinent, puritanical, Spartan; hermit, monk

example: Monks live **ascetic** lives, which draws them closer to God. They also make some really good beer!

memory word: I-said-it

picture: A wealthy man used to a life of luxury announces to his family, "I have made a decision to radically change my life and ask for your understanding and support. I am *giving up all of the comforts and luxuries* I am accustomed to for a life of discipline, meditation, and prayer. There, *I said it!*"

brevity: (brev-i-tee) **noun** – the quality or state of being brief in duration

synonyms: conciseness, pithiness, succinctness, terseness, transitory

origin: From the Latin *brevitas*, meaning "short."

example: "**Brevity** is the soul of wit," sayeth Shakespeare, meaning that a witty person can say a lot with very few words.

memory word: gravity

picture: A couple ties the knot in an unorthodox way, by having their wedding ceremony while parachuting from a plane. Before they jump, the pastor says, "Remember, this has gotta go off without a hitch. Due to *gravity*, I'll be *brief and concise*—all you have time for is 'I do.'"

candor: (kan-der) **noun** – being honest, frank, and straightforward in speech or expression

synonyms: honesty, openness, sincerity, truthfulness, veracity

origin: From the Latin *candere,* meaning "to shine, to be white."

example: Believe it or not, some politicians are no strangers to **candor**.

memory word: condor

picture: Two *condor*s, *Frank* and Earnest, stand over a rotting carcass. Earnest, savoring a mouthful of food, garbles, "Hey *Frank,* there's plenty to go around. Eat up, man." *Frank* replies, "I gotta be *honest* with you, Earnest, I'm full as a tick. I just had a steak this mornin'. I know we ain't s'posed to go around killin' our food, but sometimes I run out of patience waitin' for something to die before I can eat it. I have a freezer full of steaks and a ton of jerky at home."

despot: (**des**-puht) **noun** – a cruel, oppressive ruler with absolute power

synonyms: autocrat, dictator, oppressor, tyrant

origin: From the Greek *despotes*, meaning "master of a household, absolute ruler."

example: Hitler, Stalin, Mao, Pol Pot, and Castro are some of the most infamous **despots**.

memory word: desk-pit

picture: Dr. Evil pets his hairless Sphynx cat while sitting at his desk carrying out his *tyrannical* duties. If anyone standing in front of his desk displeases the *dictator*, he pushes a big red button, opening the trap door under their feet. You don't want to know what *cruel* creatures dwell in the *desk pit*.

malleable: (**mal**-ee-uh-buhl) **adjective** – able to be shaped or bent without breaking or cracking; easily influenced or changed

synonyms: compliant, ductile, flexible, impressionable, pliant, yielding

origin: From the Latin *malleare,* meaning "to beat with a hammer."

example: Children's minds are **malleable** like gold, able to be shaped and formed into something beautiful.

memory word: valuable

picture: An extremely wealthy man attends auctions to buy expensive things he doesn't need. Today he purchases a very *valuable* can of Crazy-Clay modeling compound (the precursor to Play-Doh) for $5,000,000. This was the very first can to roll off the assembly line back in 1920. He opens it to find that the clay is still very *pliant.*

dilatory: (dil-uh-tawr-ee) **adjective** – tending or intended to cause a delay

synonyms: dallying, lingering, putting off, tarrying, unhurried

origin: From the Latin *dilator,* meaning "procrastinator, one who delays."

example: Congress employs **dilatory** tactics because it doesn't want to deal with the sagging economy.

memory word: tell-a-story

picture: Daddy tucks Junior in at bedtime. Junior doesn't want to go to sleep yet, so he asks his father to *tell a story*. His father tells him a story, but Junior isn't satisfied. He begs for another story, and another, and another, *delaying* and *putting off* the inevitable for as long as he can.

frigid: (frij-id) **adjective** – very cold; lacking friendliness or enthusiasm

synonyms: aloof, arctic, chilly, cool, distant, frosty, standoffish

origin: From the Latin *frigidus,* meaning "cold, cool, and indifferent."

example: His greeting was as **frigid** as the cold night air.

memory word: Fridge-Ed

picture: Ed has worked at the appliance store for 30 years. He is called *Fridge Ed* because he is an expert refrigerator salesman/repairman. He couldn't care less about stoves, washers, dryers, microwaves, or any other appliances, but whenever someone comes in to buy a refrigerator or have one repaired, the staff notifies *Fridge Ed* to drop whatever he is doing so he can help the customer. This is the only time he is in a good mood. Otherwise, he is ***distant and unfriendly*** to his fellow employees and the customers.

obliterate: (uh-**blit**-uh-rayt) **verb** – to destroy completely; to delete, rub off, or erase

synonyms: annihilate, blot out, efface, eradicate, expunge, wipe out

origin: From the Latin *obliterare,* meaning "to cause to disappear, blot out, or efface."

example: Some politicians seek to undermine and **obliterate** the Constitution. As Mark Levin describes in his book *The Liberty Amendments: Restoring the American Republic,* the Founding Fathers predicted the mess we face today, and laid out a solution in Article 5 of the Constitution.

memory word: old-bitter-rake

picture: Your old rake has a few prongs missing, so you buy a new one. The old rake is jealous and bitter because it just hangs on the shed wall. In a fit of rage, the *old bitter rake* sneaks out while you are away and *completely destroys* your garden.

invert: (in-**vurt**) **verb** – to turn upside down, inside out, or reverse position of something

synonyms: flip, transpose, turn, upend, upset

origin: From the Latin *invertere,* meaning "to turn upside down."

example: When making an upside-down cake, you must place a platter over the cake mold and **invert** it to remove the cake.

memory word: it-hurts

picture: A mad scientist orders his lab assistant into a contraption he invented. The scientist closes the machine door, sets the parameters, and starts the experiment. A minute later, the door opens and his assistant emerges from a cloud of smoke. His arms and legs have *changed places*, and his head is *turned around so that he is facing backwards*. The scientist says, "Oh, my! That didn't go exactly as I had hoped. How do you feel?" His assistant groans, "*It hurts.*"

effervescent: (ef-er-**ves**-uhnt) **adjective** – excited, enthusiastic, and full of energy and high spirits; producing small bubbles of gas

synonyms: exuberant, lively, vivacious; bubbly, carbonated, fizzy

origin: From the Latin *effervescere,* meaning "to boil up, boil over."

example: A person with an **effervescent** personality often helps others feel more energized.

memory word: ever-pleasant

picture: Drink *Ever Pleasant,* the new nose-tickling, *fizzy* drink, and feel *exuberant and vivacious.*

pedestrian: (puh-**des**-tree-uhn) **adjective** – lacking in vitality or imagination; dull or commonplace; **noun** – a person who travels by foot

synonyms: banal, boring, inane, jejune, mundane, ordinary, prosaic

origin: From the Latin *pedester*, meaning "plain, not versified, prosaic; literally 'on foot'."

example: I certainly hope you find this book more interesting than other vocabulary books, which tend to be **pedestrian** and boring.

memory word: bad-equestrian

picture: An equestrian wannabe decks himself out in fancy horse-riding apparel. Since he doesn't know how to properly mount the horse, and the cinch straps on the saddle are too loose, he keeps falling off. This ***bad equestrian*** mostly just walks alongside his horse . . . ***so boring***.

infamous: (in-fuh-muhs) **adjective** – well-known for behaving badly; having a bad reputation

synonyms: contemptible, disgraceful, ignominious, notorious, villainous

origin: From the Latin *infamis,* meaning "of ill fame."

example: The **infamous** Benedict Arnold betrayed his country during the American Revolution.

memory word: infant-mouse

picture: An *infant mouse* has developed a reputation as a tough guy because of his unusual size and strength. He constantly bullies the other baby mice. This *despicable, evil, and villainous infant mouse* even intimidates the cats.

peruse: (puh-**rooz**) **verb** – to read, examine, or study in careful detail; to browse or read in a leisurely manner

synonyms: analyze, inspect, pore over, scrutinize; browse, scan, skim

example: Don't ever sign a contract until you and your attorney have **perused** it carefully. (Don't let *peruse* confuse you with its contradictory meanings. For some reason, *peruse* connotes opposites. Originally, it meant "to study carefully," but somewhere along the way it acquired the meaning "to read quickly or scan.")

memory word: bruise

picture: A bruisologist on the local CSI team **studies in detail** the color, shape, and location of **bruise**s on a victim. His **detailed inspection** with a magnifying glass helps him determine the cause and time of death.

induce: (in-**doos**) **verb** – to cause to happen; to bring about

synonyms: activate, actuate, effect, generate, produce, promote, prompt

origin: From the Latin *inducere*, meaning "to lead into, introduce."

example: Sadly, millions of adults depend on medication to **induce** sleep.

memory word: a-deuce

picture: A very pregnant queen of hearts has been in labor for too long. Her doctor says, "We can't wait any longer. Enough shuffling; it's time to deal. Let's *make this happen*." Before long, she gives birth to *a deuce* of hearts. A minute later, she births *a deuce* of spades. The doctor exclaims, "Congratulations! You have a beautiful pair of deuces there."

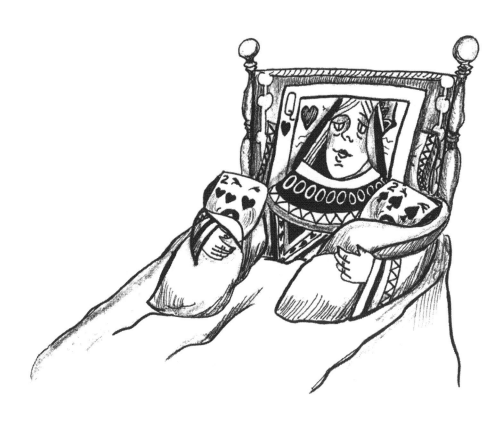

effusion: (ih-**fyoo**-zhuhn) **noun** – unrestrained expression of emotion; the flow of a liquid, gas, etc. under pressure

synonyms: gush, outburst, outflow; discharge, emission, spew, stream

origin: From the Latin *effundere,* meaning "to pour forth, spread abroad."

example: The parents had an **effusion** of praise for their four-year-old daughter's "art work."

memory word: a-few-sons

picture: A couple has one daughter and *a few sons.* Their family portrait illustrates the daughter's ***unrestrained expression of emotion*** and the sons' rather stoic demeanor.

preclude: (pri-**klood**) **verb** – to prevent something from happening or somebody from doing something; to make impossible

synonyms: avert, deter, exclude, impede, prevent, prohibit, restrain, stop

origin: From the Latin *praecludere*, meaning "to close, shut off, impede."

example: If you don't buy a lottery ticket, your decision **precludes** you from winning.

memory word: pre-glue

picture: A little boy is off to his first day of school. Anticipating severe separation anxiety from his mother, he *pre-glue*s his hand with Gooey Glue. By the time she has walked him to his classroom, the glue has set and they can't separate their hands. He *prevents* her from leaving him today, but what will he do to *avert* going to school tomorrow?

categorical: (kat-i-**gawr**-i-kuhl) **adjective** – expressed clearly, without exceptions, conditions, or reservations; pertaining to a category

synonyms: absolute, certain, definite, emphatic, positive, unequivocal

example: The schoolyard bully gave a **categorical** denial when accused of taking Jimmy's lunch money.

memory word: Cat-Oracle

picture: The crazy cat lady always consults a statue called the *Cat Oracle* when she needs to make a hard decision. It always gives an *emphatic* yes or no answer. It is *never wishy-washy* with its response.

benefactor: (**ben**-uh-fak-ter) **noun** – a person who gives financial help to organizations such as schools or charities

synonyms: altruist, humanitarian, patron, philanthropist, sponsor

origin: *Benefactor* comes from the Latin phrase *bene facere,* meaning "to do well." *Bene* means "well" and *facere* means "to do."

example: The United States of America has long been a **benefactor** to the world. The U.S. is often the first to offer help when a disaster occurs.

memory word: Ben-A.-Factor

picture: You present an award to *Ben A. Factor,* the most *charitable and giving person* in your community. He has given millions to schools, various charities, and scholarship foundations. He's definitely *been a factor* in the life of the community.

illicit: (ih-**lis**-it) **adjective** – not legally permitted or authorized; not approved of by the normal morals or ethics of society

synonyms: criminal, felonious, forbidden, illegal, immoral, unlawful

origin: From the Latin *illicitus,* meaning "not allowed, unlawful, illegal."

example: The 18th Amendment to the U.S. Constitution outlawed liquor, spurring one of the largest **illicit** black markets—bootlegging.

memory word: eel-is-it

picture: In 1933, Albert Einstein is leaving Germany as Hitler comes to power. It is *illegal* to take certain items out of the country. Einstein, trying to smuggle an electric eel, makes his way through customs. Hitler personally searches his luggage. He discovers the electric eel and says, "An *eel is it?*" He shocks Einstein with the eel, confiscates it, and sends Einstein on his way.

affluent: (af-loo-uhnt) **adjective** – having an abundance of wealth

synonyms: loaded, prosperous, rich, upscale, well off, well-to-do

origin: From the Latin *affluens,* meaning "abounding, rich, plentiful."

example: Prosperous families live in **affluent** neighborhoods.

memory word: a-flute

picture: The *richest* person in the world sits on top of a pile of money playing *a flute*. Instead of emitting music, money pours out of the flute.

flaccid: (**flas**-id) **adjective** – lacking firmness, hardness, or elasticity

synonyms: drooping, flabby, flimsy, lax, limp, loose, slack, soft, weak

origin: From the Latin *flaccus,* meaning "flabby, flap-eared."

example: The **flaccid** stalks of celery have been in the refrigerator much too long.

memory word: flask-lid

picture: A student in the science lab doesn't follow instructions. One day, he thinks, "What if?" and mixes some chemicals just to see what happens. He places the lid on the flask and shakes it up. Fortunately for him and everyone else, he doesn't blow up the lab. However, the *flask lid loses its firmness,* goes *limp,* drops into the flask, and dissolves.

haphazard: (hap-**haz**-erd) **adjective** – characterized by a lack of order or planning; determined by randomness or chance

synonyms: aimless, erratic, helter-skelter, indiscriminate, random

example: Even though the layout of the absent-minded professor's office appeared **haphazard**, he knew the exact location of every paper and book.

memory word: hat-hazard

picture: Imagine a gargantuan man *aimlessly* walking down the sidewalk. As he walks, he yanks his hat off his head and tosses it up in the air without a care where the monstrous thing will land. As quickly as he removes one hat and discards it, another one appears on his head. He repeats the process, littering the storefronts with his hats. Wherever one lands, it creates a *hat hazard*.

allege: (uh-**lej**) **verb** – to state something as fact without proof

synonyms: assert, charge, maintain, present, profess, put forward

origin: From the Latin *allegare,* meaning "to bring forth, produce in evidence."

example: Billy never made an A on a test in his life, so when he scored an A+ on his math test, the other students **alleged** that he cheated.

memory word: a-ledge

picture: You work in a high-rise office building. One day, you hear a loud siren and shout, "There's a jumper out on *a ledge!*" Because of your over-active imagination, you assume it is a fire truck coming to the rescue and *state it as fact without proof.*

indulge: (in-**duhlj**) **verb** – to yield to a desire; to take unrestrained pleasure in

synonyms: allow, give in, gratify, satiate, spoil, yield

origin: From the Latin *indulgere*, meaning "to pamper, permit, gratify."

example: Universal law dictates the following (especially if you are over 40): **indulge** your sweet tooth and you will bulge.

memory word: bulge

picture: You enter a bakery and *give into your desire* for all of the goodies. You indulge until you *bulge*.

stoic: (**stoh**-ik) **adjective** – not affected by or showing passion or feeling; **noun** – a person who accepts what happens without complaining or showing emotion

synonyms: calm, detached, indifferent, self-controlled, unemotional

example: Many characters played by Clint Eastwood are **stoic** tough guys. (Stoicism, an ancient Greek philosophy, teaches that reason can overcome destructive emotions resulting from errors in judgment. A person who attains moral and intellectual perfection will lead a virtuous life.)

memory word: toe-itch

picture: Everyone on the football team suffers from a horrible case of athlete's foot, even the guy who thinks of himself as a *stoic*. As his teammates maniacally scratch their *toe itch* in the locker room, he dons his uniform and heads out to the field. Whistling cheerfully, he *displays complete indifference* to the irritable itching.

tout: (tout) **verb** – to praise, advertise, or publicize highly and boastfully

synonyms: acclaim, herald, laud, plug, proclaim, promote, trumpet

example: The media **touts** the mop-haired boy band as the next Beatles.

memory word: trout

picture: A whale of a *trout* catches you and dangles you by your feet for everyone to see. The *trout* shouts through a megaphone, *proclaiming* its great accomplishment.

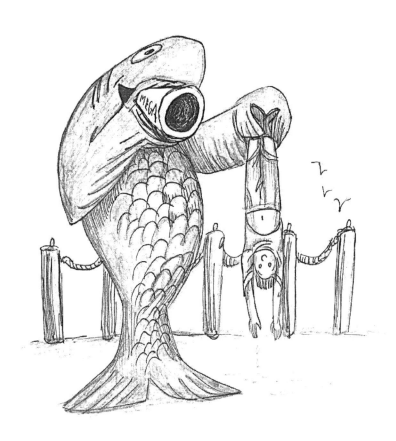

bereft: (bih-**reft**) **adjective** – lacking something needed, wanted, or expected; sad because of the loss of something or someone

synonyms: bereaved, deprived, destitute, dispossessed, wanting

example: He was **bereft** when his girlfriend broke up with him.

memory word: bee-raft

picture: Several large bees have been shipwrecked and are now *lost*, drifting on a raft without a sail or paddles. Their plight makes them *sorrowful and sad*. I wouldn't want to be a bee on that *bee raft!*

ambience: (**am**-bee-uhns) **noun** – the character and atmosphere of an environment

synonyms: climate, environs, feeling, mood, surroundings

origin: From the Latin *ambire,* meaning "to surround, encompass."

example: She turned out the lights, lit some candles, and played Mozart to create just the right **ambience**.

memory word: ambulance

picture: Every time an *ambulance* speeds down the road, its loud siren creates a *mood and atmosphere* that upsets the drivers who have pulled over to let it pass. I always say a prayer for the safety of the first responders and whomever they are on their way to help.

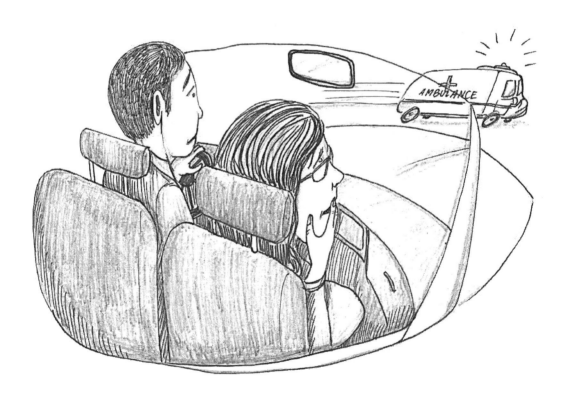

uniform: (**yoo**-nuh-fawrm) **adjective** – the same throughout in structure, composition, or detail; identical or consistent

synonyms: homogeneous, standardized, undeviating, unvarying

origin: From the Latin *uniformis,* meaning "having one form."

example: The SAT and ACT are **uniform** tests that juniors and seniors take in high school to assess their academic readiness for college.

memory word: unicorn

picture: A *unicorn* skates in a perfect figure 8 on a frozen lake. It *does not deviate or vary* from the *unchanging* figure 8.

potent: (**poht**-nt) **adjective** – possessing great strength, influence, or authority; having a powerful physiological or chemical effect

synonyms: compelling, dominant, mighty, robust, strong, vigorous

origin: From the Latin *potens,* meaning "powerful, mighty, effectual."

example: The witch brewed a **potent** potion.

memory word: pole-tent

picture: A *pole* holds up a large circus *tent*. It flexes its *strong* muscles, bragging, "I can hold up this tent all by myself!"

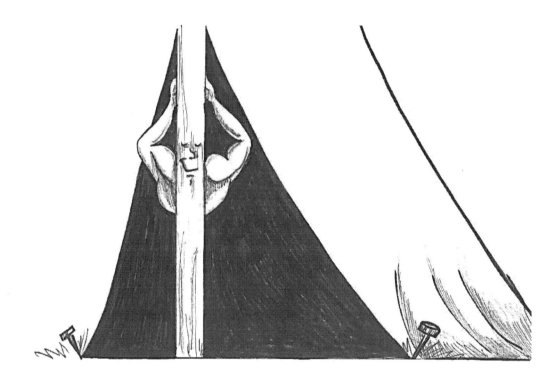

malicious: (muh-**lish**-uhs) **adjective** – motivated by hateful, vicious, or mischievous purposes with the desire to harm someone or hurt their feelings

synonyms: malevolent, pernicious, spiteful, vengeful, vicious, wicked

origin: From the Latin *malus,* meaning "bad."

example: Some people use social media for no other reason than to spread **malicious** gossip, rumors, and lies.

memory word: delicious

picture: A *mean and vicious* coworker offers you a chocolate cake, saying "Let's start over and bury the hatchet." With a Cheshire grin on his face, he presents the *delicious* chocolate cake made with lots of Ex-Lax.

amity: (am-i-tee) **noun** – a friendly and harmonious relationship between people or countries

synonyms: comity, concord, cordiality, friendliness, goodwill, harmony

origin: From the Latin *amicus*, meaning "friend."

example: If everyone gave and received unconditional love, the world would be filled with **amity**.

memory word: Emmitt-E.

picture: Everyone has heard of Casper, the *friendly* ghost. Did you know that he has a brother named *Emmitt E.*, the *cordial* ghost? Oddly enough, he lives in *harmony* with a squad of ghostbusters.

contend: (kuhn-**tend**) **verb** – to maintain or assert something is true, especially in an argument; to compete, as in a contest or game

synonyms: contest, dispute, skirmish, vie

origin: From the Latin *contendere,* meaning "to stretch out, strive after."

example: You might disagree with me, but I **contend** that the bigger our government gets, the more our freedoms dwindle.

memory word: con-ten

picture: Ten convicts argue over whose gang is the toughest. The five on one side *assert* they are the baddest around and the five on the other side *maintain* the opposite. After a round of insults, the *con ten* decide to settle the issue with a friendly *contest* of tug of war.

negligent: (neg-li-juhnt) **adjective** – failure to give enough care or attention; having an undue lack of concern with detrimental results

synonyms: derelict, inattentive, neglectful, thoughtless, unconcerned

origin: From the Latin *negligens*, meaning "unconcerned, careless."

example: Drunk drivers are grossly **negligent** and scofflaws.

memory word: negligee

picture: You work at a *negligee* store and are in charge of closing the store. Last night, you *carelessly* forgot to lock the door and set the alarm. The employee opening the store the next morning discovered that, due to your *neglect*, someone had stolen all of the merchandise.

phlegmatic: (fleg-**mat**-ik) **adjective** – not easily excited to action or display of emotion

synonyms: apathetic, emotionless, sluggish, unexcitable, unresponsive

origin: From the Greek *phlegma,* meaning "humor caused by heat."

example: The federal government is a **phlegmatic**, unresponsive, and bureaucratic juggernaut.

memory word: flag-medic

picture: A U.S. flag that doubles as a medic on an EMT crew checks the vital signs of an *unresponsive* victim. The *flag medic* needs to determine if it is safe to turn the victim over and start CPR.

cursory: (**kur**-suh-ree) **adjective** – quickly and incompletely done, without paying attention to details

synonyms: desultory, hasty, hurried, perfunctory, quick, superficial

origin: From the Latin *currere*, meaning "to run." (The straight up-and-down line blinking on your computer monitor to indicate the position on the page is called a cursor. *Cursor* is Latin for "runner." Hence, the cursor runs across the screen.)

example: While some museum patrons study each artifact carefully, others give **cursory** glances and move on to the next thing.

memory word: curse-Ory

picture: Ory's friend texts him, asking if he can meet the gang at the movie theater. His mom says he can go after he cleans his room. So he sweeps the dirt under the rug, sloppily makes his bed, and crams his dirty clothes under the bed. He does the job *quickly and incompletely* because he doesn't want to miss the movie. His mom notices the *superficial* cleaning job only after he leaves. She says to herself, "Well, *curse Ory*. That stinker."

stymie: (**stahy**-mee) **verb** – to hinder or prevent the progress or accomplishment of

synonyms: confound, foil, frustrate, impede, obstruct, stonewall, thwart

example: Each of her moves **stymied** the plan for his next Scrabble word.

memory word: sty-me

picture: A humongous sty in a pirate's eye *obstructs* his view. "Arrggh," he says. "I've a sty in me eye. I'll never find that white whale with a patch on one eye and a *sty* in *me* other."

translucent: (trans-**loo**-suhnt) **adjective** – permitting light to pass through, but diffusing it so objects on the other side are not clearly visible

synonyms: pellucid, semi-opaque, semi-transparent, translucid

origin: From the Latin *translucere,* meaning "to shine through."

example: Many sea creatures, such as jellyfish and glass shrimp, are **translucent**.

memory word: train-Lou-sent

picture: Uncle Lou sends another rare and unusual toy train to his nephew, a toy train enthusiast. The nephew holds the *train Lou sent* up to the light, exclaiming, "Cool! I can *almost see through* it."

unkempt: (uhn-**kempt**) **adjective** – not properly maintained or cared for; not combed

synonyms: disheveled, grungy, messy, neglected, slovenly, unpolished

example: My lawn is meticulously kept during the summer, but **unkempt** and messy during the winter, when it is too cold to spend time outdoors.

memory word: nun-kept

picture: Nuns are known for their neatness and orderliness, but Sister Mary *Slovenly* is an exception. Because she did *not properly maintain* her room at the convent, they kicked her out. The *nun kept neglecting* her *grungy* quarters.

wither: (**with**-her) **verb** – to dry or shrivel up; to lose freshness, strength, vigor, or vitality

synonyms: atrophy, desiccate; decay, deteriorate, languish, shrink, wilt

example: Those who remain active in their old age don't **wither** away as quickly as those who neglect their health.

memory word: weather

picture: Slices of fruit in a dehydrator complain about the *wilting* heat. An apple slice says to a banana slice, "We're going to *shrivel up* and die if this *weather* keeps up."

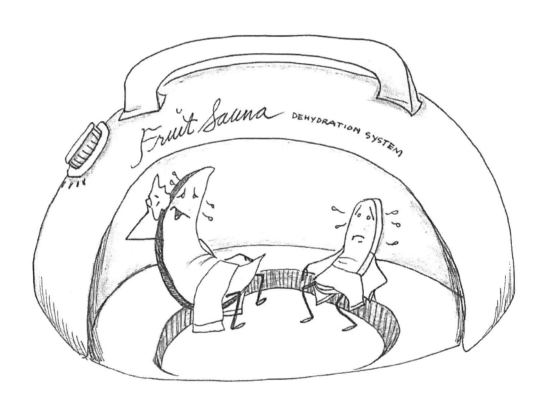

intermittent: (in-ter-**mit**-nt) **adjective** – alternately starting and stopping at regular or irregular intervals

synonyms: irregular, occasional, periodic, rhythmic, sporadic

origin: From the Latin *intermittere*, meaning "to leave an interval."

example: Lightning strikes are **intermittent** and unpredictable.

memory word: enter-mitten

picture: You work in quality control at a bottle factory. You *randomly* select bottles as they pass by on the conveyor belt, inspecting them for uniformity in color, thickness, and for cosmetic flaws. One day, someone plays a joke on you; or maybe your supervisor is checking to see if you are paying attention. *Periodically*, a bottle will go by with a furry mitten slipped over it. There's no set pattern, but this happens often enough to keep you on your toes. Just when you think there will be no more, *enter mitten*.

eclectic: (ih-**klek**-tik) **adjective** – selecting or from various sources

synonyms: diverse, mingled, mixed, selective, varied, wide-ranging

origin: From the Greek *eklektikos*, meaning "selective, picking out."

example: Amy has an **eclectic** taste in music. She likes several genres, including classical, rock, rap, country, and folk.

memory word: egg-lick-tick

picture: An egg engages in a carefully *selective*, yet odd, process of choosing a pet at the pet store. It licks each pet to determine if it is the right one or not. Finally, *egg lick*s a *tick* and says, "I love them all, but this is the one! Put a leash on him and I'll take him home." He says to the tick, "I'm going to name you Tack-Toe…he he he!"

infer: (in-**fur**) **verb** – to reach a conclusion, judgment, or decision on the basis of available information

synonyms: conjecture, deduce, derive, presume, speculate, surmise

origin: From the Latin *inferre,* meaning "to bring into; to deduce, conclude."

example: You come home from school and the TV is on, mom's car is in the driveway, and her purse is on the kitchen table. Even though she is nowhere in sight, you can safely **infer** she is home.

memory word: in-fur

picture: A group of cavemen wake up one morning to find one of their hairy-knuckled friends missing. They call in Zog, the detective, to solve the mystery. After collecting evidence, the caveman detective declares, "Based on information Zog find, and this note me find *in fur* coat pocket of missing knuckle-dragger, me *deduce*…" At that moment, a stalactite falls and hits him on the head, killing him. The mystery remains unsolved.

portent: (**pohr**-tent) **noun** – a sign or indication of something momentous about to happen, especially something negative

synonyms: foreboding, foreshadowing, harbinger, omen, premonition

origin: From the Latin *portentum*, meaning "a sign, token, omen."

example: Comets have been considered **portents** of both good and bad events throughout history.

memory word: poor-tint

picture: You have your car windows tinted. A week later, you see an *indication or sign* that they did a *poor tint* job. Tiny bubbles appear and grow larger each day.

obsolete: (ob-suh-**leet**) **adjective** – no longer in use or practice; out of date or outmoded

synonyms: ancient, antiquated, antique, archaic, old, old-fashioned

origin: From the Latin *obsoletus*, meaning "grown old, worn out."

example: Antique stores are filled with many **obsolete** items, such as Polaroid cameras and vinyl record players.

memory word: I'm-so-late

picture: You show up late for your new job because you ride an *old-fashioned* bicycle (Hi-Wheel) with a ridiculously huge wheel in front. "I'm sorry *I'm so late!*" you say. "My transportation is *outdated*. I'm donating it to a museum after work today, and then I'm upgrading."

turbulent: (**tur**-byuh-luhnt) **adjective** – characterized by unrest or disorder; marked by vigorous agitation or a violent disturbance of a liquid or gas

synonyms: agitated, inclement, stormy, tempestuous, tumultuous

origin: From the Latin *turbulentus*, meaning "full of commotion."

example: Aircraft are designed to withstand **turbulent** conditions.

memory word: turban-lint

picture: Two men sit next to each other during a *tumultuous* flight. One wears a white turban, the other a black turban. During a particularly *violent disturbance*, the passengers are bounced around and covered with debris. The men are angry because the white turban is covered with black *turban lint* and the black turban is covered with white *turban lint*.

mellifluous: (muh-lif-loo-uhs) **adjective** – a smoothly flowing sound or voice

synonyms: dulcet, euphonic, harmonic, mellow, pleasing, soothing

origin: From the Latin *mel* (honey), and *fluus* (flowing), meaning "flowing with honey." (The name *Mel*issa means "honeybee.")

example: The singer with the most **mellifluous** voice won the contest.

memory word: Mel-if-Louis

picture: The Tonstrina Quattor (Latin for the Barbershop Four) is a barbershop quartet on tour. TQ's tenor, Louis, has laryngitis. The others are wondering what they will do without Louis's *smooth* voice. One says, "We'll have to call his brother *Mel, if Louis* isn't ready for our next performance."

extricate: (ek-stri-kayt) **verb** – to free or release from entanglement, a trap, or a difficult situation

synonyms: disentangle, extract, liberate, loosen, release, remove, rescue

origin: From the Latin *extricare*, meaning "to disentangle, unravel."

example: First responders sometimes use a tool called the Jaws of Life to **extricate** crash victims from their vehicles.

memory word: extra-cape

picture: While trying to catch the bad guy and save the day, a klutzy superhero snags his cape on something and tears the cloth while trying to *extract it*. That's why he always carries an ***extra cape***.

distended: (dih-**sten**-did) **adjective** – increased in size or volume; swollen because of pressure from inside

synonyms: bloated, bulging, inflated, puffed out, tumescent, turgid

origin: From the Latin *distendere*, meaning "to swell or stretch out."

example: Eat a large pizza all by yourself and drink a two-liter bottle of soda; then you'll appreciate the full meaning of **distended**.

memory word: this-tender

picture: A daredevil working on a movie full of stupid stunts hopes to surpass the success of the *Jackass* movies. He breaks nearly every bone in his body. In the emergency room, the doctor pokes his *swollen* body several times in different places asking, "Is ***this tender?***"

poignant: (**poin**-yuhnt) **adjective** – sharply distressing or painful to the feelings; keen or strong in mental appeal; to the point

synonyms: agonizing, emotional, heartrending, sorrowful, touching

origin: From the Latin *pungere*, meaning "to prick, pierce, sting."

example: The scene where Forrest Gump meets the son he didn't know he had is very **poignant**.

memory word: coin-hunt

picture: A miserable-looking homeless person holds a cardboard sign at an intersection. While he waits for the next red light, he busily searches for coins along the sidewalk. A millionaire observes this *coin hunt* and is *deeply moved*. Rolling down his window, he hands the homeless man his business card and a bag of gold coins and says, "Call me. There's more where that came from!"

mitigate: (**mit**-i-gayt) **verb** – to lessen the seriousness, severity, intensity, or extent of

synonyms: alleviate, blunt, ease, extenuate, moderate, palliate, reduce

origin: From the Latin *mitigare*, meaning "to soften, ripen, mellow."

example: Proper ergonomics and frequent stretch breaks help **mitigate** the negative effects of sitting at a computer all day, every day.

memory word: middle-gate

picture: Three gates lead into Hell. The two outer gates look menacing and are engulfed in flames. Unexpectedly, a red carpet leads to the *middle gate*, which is lined with delicious food and drink and thousands of massage therapists, who give free ten-minute chair massages to everyone! The approach to the *middle gate* is thus designed to *lessen the severity* of the descent into Hell. That's a relief!

glib: (glib) **adjective** – artfully persuasive in speech that is often superficial or insincere

synonyms: eloquent, fast-talking, slippery, suave, urbane

example: Fast-talking politicians are commonly referred to as **glib**.

memory word: rib

picture: You study the purpose and function of the human *rib* in your anatomy and physiology textbook. The *rib* in the picture comes to life, popping out of your book and giving you a short lecture. Although it *speaks eloquently*, the *rib* is *slippery* and repeatedly slides off the book onto the desk.

foist: (foist) **verb** – to force someone to accept something that is not wanted

synonyms: compel, fob off, impose, insert

example: Congress, well-known for **foisting** burdensome laws and regulations on us, exempts itself from those same laws.

memory word: roast

picture: A man comes home from work to find the two-year-old triplets creating sheer bedlam. Mom is dressed up for a night out on the town. She *forces* a pot *roast* into his hands, telling him to warm it up for dinner. She *imposes* this chore on him because she is ready to snap and needs an evening out with her girlfriends.

antipathy: (an-**tip**-uh-thee) **noun** – a strong feeling of dislike

synonyms: animosity, aversion, enmity, hostility, loathing, rancor

origin: From the Greek *antipatheia*, meaning "having opposite feeling."

example: Some people love cats, but others loathe them with enormous **antipathy**.

memory word: ant-tip-of-tree

picture: An ant at the top of a tree *strongly dislikes* the other ants on the ground and can't get far enough away. He sticks out his tongue and shakes his fist with furious *rancor*. One of the ants on the ground points to the *ant* on the *tip of* the *tree*, musing to the others, "Check him out. Why is he so *hostile*? What's his problem?"

egalitarian: (ih-gal-i-**tair**-ee-uhn) **adjective** – characterized by belief in equal economic, political, and social rights for all people; **noun** – one who holds this belief

synonyms: equitable, impartial, just, unbiased

origin: From the Latin *aequalitas*, meaning "equality, likeness."

example: Some politicians say they want an **egalitarian** society, yet they pass laws rewarding one constituency while punishing another.

memory word: eagle-tearing

picture: KKK members plaster posters all over town advertising their upcoming march against Jews, blacks, and Catholics. As fast as the Klan can put the posters up, they see an *eagle tearing* them down.

ostensible: (o-**sten**-suh-buhl) **adjective** – represented or outwardly appearing as such

synonyms: alleged, apparent, evident, professed, purported, seeming

origin: From the Latin *ostendere*, meaning "to show, expose to view."

example: A person's true motivation might not always be the **ostensible** one. For instance, calling in sick might just be an excuse to stay home and watch movies all day.

memory word: a-stinking-bull

picture: You attend a baseball game. A few minutes after taking your seat, you smell a horrible odor. The man in the seat to your right is dirty and unkempt. It *seems evident* that he is the source. To your surprise, he stands up to leave in the middle of the game, blurting out, "I can't stand the stench any longer!" You look around, attempting to locate the source, and find *a stinking bull* sitting directly behind you.

derogate: (**der**-uh-gayt) **verb** – to cause to seem inferior; to take away a part so as to impair the whole; to disparage or belittle

synonyms: denigrate, detract, discredit, disparage, insult, slander

origin: From the Latin *derogare*, meaning "to take away, detract from."

example: Jealous of the head cheerleader, she started spreading rumors to **derogate** her reputation.

memory word: dirt-on-gate

picture: The Smiths desperately try to keep up with their next-door neighbors, the Joneses. The Joneses put up a shiny new stainless steel gate for their front yard fence. Mr. Smith kicks *dirt on* the *gate* to *detract from* its good looks, because his gate now seems *inferior*.

sacrosanct: (sak-roh-sangkt) **adjective** – regarded as sacred and protected by law, custom, or respect

synonyms: consecrated, hallowed, holy, sacramental, sanctified

origin: From the Latin *sacrosanctus*, meaning "consecrated with religious ceremonies."

example: Some men, including this author, consider their garages to be **sacrosanct**.

memory word: sack-rolls-sank

picture: A sack, out for a stroll with his family, saw the Reflecting Pool between the Lincoln Memorial and the Washington Monument and said, "Hey, look, kids! A swimming pool!" The *sack roll*ed in, *sank,* and then resurfaced. His wife scolded, "Get out of there right this instant! That is a *hallowed* reflecting pool, NOT a swimming pool!"

coalesce: (koh-uh-**les**) **verb** – to unite or come together in some manner

synonyms: amalgamate, cleave, cohere, conjoin, consolidate, fuse, merge

origin: From the Latin *coalescere*, meaning "to unite, grow together."

example: A university campus is a place where young people from different backgrounds **coalesce** to party.

memory word: cold-S

picture: A bunch of S's outside in the freezing cold *come together* around a fire to keep warm. Members of the *cold S* group take turns gathering wood to stoke the fire.

legacy: (leg-uh-see) **noun** – a gift by will, such as money or property; something handed down from an ancestor or a predecessor

synonyms: bequest, birthright, endowment, heritage, inheritance

origin: From the Latin *legare*, meaning "to appoint by a last will, send as a legate."

example: Due to the greed, incompetence, and negligence of Congress, future generations must pay for its **legacy** of massive debt.

memory word: leg-you-see

picture: Your father *bequeaths* a box of keepsakes to you. The first thing you pull out of the box? It's a *leg you see*.

broach: (brohch) **verb** – to bring up a topic for discussion, usually a difficult one due to its embarrassing or stressful nature

synonyms: introduce, mention, propose, raise, suggest

origin: From the Latin *broccus*, meaning "projecting, pointed."

example: While driving home, Junior fretted how to **broach** the subject of the new dent on his dad's car.

memory word: roach

picture: Huge roaches in a dark, smoky room sit around a table in silence, staring at each other. Finally, the *roach* at the head of the table *introduces the subject for discussion*. He croaks, "I've called you all here to discuss our options with this pesky Roach Terminator Man."

incoherent: (in-koh-**heer**-uhnt) **adjective** – without logical or meaningful connection; not clear and hard to understand

synonyms: inarticulate, muddled, mumbling, rambling, wandering

example: Grief, anger, or even joy can render one temporarily **incoherent**.

memory word: ink-on-hairy-ant

picture: An immense hairy ant, covered with purple ink, tries to speak to you, but its tongue is tied in a knot. You find it *impossible to understand* what the purple ant is trying to say. As it approaches, you turn and run so the *ink on hairy ant* won't ruin your clothes.

amiable: (**ay**-mee-uh-buhl) **adjective** – having or displaying a pleasant or agreeable nature; easy to get along with

synonyms: affable, engaging, friendly, genial, gracious, sociable

origin: From the Latin *amicas*, meaning "friend."

example: As a rule of thumb, people who smile a lot are very **amiable**.

memory word: ham-eating-bull

picture: An *engaging* bull, eating a ham hock, laughs and enjoys the company of his *friends*. You've never seen a ***ham-eating bull?***

neophyte: (**nee**-uh-fahyt) **noun** – a person who has recently started an activity; a new convert to a religion

synonyms: amateur, apprentice, freshman, greenhorn, novice, rookie

origin: From the Greek *neophytos*, meaning "new convert."

example: You are a **neophyte** if the idea of using mnemonics to quickly and permanently memorize vocabulary words is new to you. By the time you finish this book, you will be an expert.

memory word: Neil-fight

picture: Neil takes up cage fighting. During his first fight, his opponent chases him around the cage. His friends shout, *"Neil! Fight! Stop running and fight!"* Neil shouts back, "But I'm just a *beginner!* This guy's gonna kill me!"

rotund: (roh-**tuhnd**) **adjective** – round in shape; plump or fat

synonyms: burly, chunky, dumpy, hefty, obese, portly, tubby

origin: From the Latin *rotundus*, meaning "round, spherical."

example: Santa Claus and his sack of presents are both **rotund.**

memory word: row-ton

picture: A 2,000-pound *portly* man rows a boat. A couple of less *hefty* fishermen on the pier watch him row by. One says to the other, "That's not something you see every day. I wouldn't have thought anyone could *row* a *ton* of his own weight."

subjugate: (**suhb**-juh-gayt) **verb** – to bring under complete control; to make submissive or subservient

synonyms: conquer, enslave, force, overcome, quell, rule, subdue, tame

example: History is filled with examples of one nation **subjugating** another. In fact, ancient Rome's motto was *Divide et Impera*, meaning "Divide and Conquer."

memory word: sub-jug-ate

picture: An old jug eats a sub sandwich every day. Around noon, the jug mounts its horse and rides out on the range, where it lassos a fresh sub. Once the jug *subdues* the sub, it slings it over its shoulder and heads back to the ranch house, where it eats the sub. Today's sub is exceptional. It is the all-time best *sub jug ate*.

deplete: (dih-**pleet**) **verb** – to critically decrease or exhaust the abundance or supply of

synonyms: bankrupt, diminish, drain, empty, expend, use up, weaken

origin: From the Latin *deplere*, meaning "to empty."

example: A drought will **deplete** an area's water source, necessitating water rationing.

memory word: the-bleep

picture: A man is late for work because his son borrowed the car last night and left the headlights on, *draining* the battery. After a jump from his neighbor, he stops for gas because his son left an *empty* tank. By the time he arrives at the office, everyone has already *finished* the coffee and donuts. A co-worker borrows his tape and stapler and *uses up* both of them. After work, the man stops at an ATM before meeting his friends for drinks, only to discover that his account is *bankrupt*. Because he doesn't have any money, his friends buy him a beer. He takes one sip and then goes to the restroom. When he returns, he finds that someone *drained* his beer. At this point he loses it and shouts, "What *the bleep!* Who drank my beer?"

composure: (kuhm-**poh**-zher) **noun** – steadiness of mind under stress

synonyms: aplomb, calm, control, cool, equanimity, poise, self-assurance

example: James Bond never loses his **composure**, even in the most impossible and dangerous situations.

memory word: calm-poser

picture: Bodybuilders are posing on stage when someone yells "Fire!" All of a sudden, pandelirium ensues (I know that's not a word, but it should be). Everyone screams, scrambling for the exits—except for the *calm poser*. He behaves as if nothing is wrong, proceeding through the poses he practiced for weeks in *a calm and controlled state of mind*.

aphorism: (af-uh-riz-uhm) **noun** – a short saying embodying a general truth or astute observation

synonyms: adage, axiom, maxim, moral, precept, proverb, saying, truism

origin: From the Greek *aphorismos*, meaning "definition, pithy sentence."

example: An **aphorism** is a wise saying that, if held deeply and practiced, enriches one's life. For example: "He who opens a school door, closes a prison" or "Necessity is the mother of invention."

memory word: apple-rhythm

picture: A giant apple holds a Bible opened to the Book of Proverbs. Reading the wise *precepts* aloud, it taps its foot to the rhythm and sings the *truisms* in the *proverbs*. The *apple rhythm* is kinda catchy.

polemic: (puh-**lem**-ik) **noun** – a strongly written or spoken attack against someone else's opinions, beliefs, or practices; a person who makes an aggressive argument

synonyms: argument, contention, refutation; quarreler

example: Watch any political talk show and you will witness nonstop **polemics** that usually devolve into *ad hominem* attacks.

memory word: anemic

picture: Your mother's doctor runs a lot of tests because she is weak and tired all the time. He determines that she needs bypass heart surgery—ASAP! She seeks a second opinion from another doctor, who *strongly refutes* the first doctor's diagnosis and *quarrels* with his methods. He calls him a second-rate quack, asking sarcastically, "Where did he get his license—from a Cracker Jack box?" He reassures your mother that she is simply *anemic* and needs to supplement her diet with more iron.

labyrinth: (**lab**-uh-rinth) **noun** – a complex system of paths, passages, or tunnels in which it is easy to lose one's way

synonyms: jungle, maze, morass, network, perplexity, puzzle, web

example: The IRS tax code is a **labyrinth** of rules and regulations nearly impossible to navigate.

memory word: lab-rat

picture: An elephantine *lab rat* works his way through an immense *maze*, navigating the ***network of twists and turns*** as he seeks his delectable reward at the end…YOU!

empirical: (em-**pir**-i-kuhl) **adjective** – derived from or relating to experiment and observation rather than theory

synonyms: data-based, factual, firsthand, observed, practical, pragmatic

example: Man-made global warming is mere conjecture at this point. Over 9,000 scientists claim that **empirical** evidence disproves the global warming hoax.

memory word: pierced-skull

picture: You trek through the Amazon rain forest with your guide Quiqueg, who tells frightening stories about the head shrinkers in the jungle. You don't believe these people really exist; you think he's just trying to scare you. Then you encounter a tribe of head shrinkers *firsthand* and see the *pierced skull*s hanging around their necks. You worry that your once-in-a-lifetime adventure is about to be cut short.

incisive: (in-**sahy**-siv) **adjective** – very clear and direct, able to explain difficult ideas clearly and confidently; adapted for cutting or piercing

synonyms: acute, concise, cutting, keen, penetrating, profound, sharp

origin: From the Latin *incidere*, meaning "to cut."

example: Emily is known for her **incisive** mind and quick wit.

memory word: incisor

picture: Imagine a mouth with pronounced *incisors* (buck teeth). The *sharp incisors* bite into an apple with a worm and the poor little guy is *cut* in half.

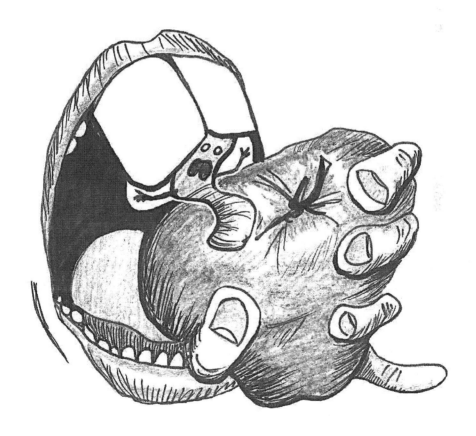

forbear: (fawr-**bair**) **verb** – to refrain or abstain from doing or saying something

synonyms: bridle, curb, desist, eschew, forgo, hold back, inhibit, restrain

example: It is wise to **forbear** speaking your mind when you are extremely upset.

memory word: four-bears

picture: While camping, you wake up one night to a rustling sound outside your tent. You peek out and see *four bears* rummaging through your stuff. Needless to say, you *refrain* from interrupting them while they eat all of your food. Patience is a virtue, and in this case it can help you live longer, too.

comity: (**kom**-i-tee) **noun** – a state or atmosphere of harmony, mutual civility, respect, and courtesy among people, organizations, and nations

synonyms: concord, congeniality, fellowship, oneness, peace, solidarity

origin: From the Latin *comitas*, meaning "courtesy, friendliness."

example: This word is often used in the phrase "**comity** of nations," meaning courteous respect by one nation for the laws of another.

memory word: committee

picture: Representatives from various countries meet in a *committee* to discuss solutions to conflicts around the globe. Despite their differing religions, cultures, and traditions, they enjoy *an atmosphere of harmony.*

paucity: (**paw**-si-tee) **noun** – an insufficient quantity of something

synonyms: dearth, deficiency, insufficiency, scantiness, scarcity, shortage

origin: From the Latin *paucus*, meaning "few, little."

example: There is a **paucity** of honest politicians in Washington, D.C.

memory word: paw-city

picture: *Paw City*, founded many years ago by a group of grizzly bears, today is a ghost town due to the *scarcity* of salmon in the river. The river dried up after a dam was built upstream, so the grizzlies had to move on.

appease: (uh-**peez**) **verb** – to bring to a state of peace, quiet, or contentment; to satisfy, allay, or relieve; to yield or concede to the belligerent demands of a person, group, or nation

synonyms: assuage, conciliate, ease, gratify, mollify, placate, soothe

example: Although expensive, the "bread and circuses" of ancient Rome succeeded in **appeasing** and pacifying the masses.

memory word: up-heaves

picture: Moments before a secret agent is captured by the enemy, he swallows the thumb drive holding top secret files. After unceasing interrogation and torture, he decides to ***concede to their demands*** and give them what they want. So he ***up heaves*** the thumb drive and says, "Here, everything you want is on this."

gregarious: (gri-**gair**-ee-uhs) **adjective** – fond of the companionship of others; living in flocks or herds

synonyms: affable, extroverted, outgoing, sociable

origin: From the Latin *grex*, meaning "flock, herd, swarm, pack."

example: Solitary confinement could arguably be considered the ultimate punishment for a **gregarious** person.

memory word: Greg-Airhead

picture: *Greg Airhead* is very *sociable*. His bulbous balloon head is filled with helium. At the high school dance, he floats from group to group, *enjoying their company*.

kinetic: (ki-**net**-ik) **adjective** – of or produced by movement

synonyms: active, animated, dynamic, lively, spirited, tireless, vivacious

example: Electricity can be created by the **kinetic** energy of water flowing through a hydroelectric plant within a dam, or by the wind that turns the turbines in a windmill.

memory word: can-attic

picture: No one in your family can sleep at night because a huge metal can in the attic is in *constant motion* and constantly bumping into things. Its *tireless* movement produces a cacophony that earplugs can't block out. The household beneath the *can attic* could use a good night of sleep.

mollify: (**mol**-uh-fahy) **verb** – to cause to be more favorably inclined; to lessen the harshness or severity of

synonyms: ameliorate, appease, assuage, mitigate, pacify, placate, soften

origin: From the Latin *mollificare*, meaning "to make soft."

example: The waiter tried to **mollify** the customer, but to no avail; he is a malcontent who looks for every excuse not to leave a tip.

memory word: mall-if-I

picture: A man says to his wife, "I'll clean the whole house, wax your car, and take you power shopping at the *mall if I* can get out of the "dog house." If nothing else works, the power shopping should *appease* her and end his time in the dog house.

nostalgic: (no-**stal**-jik) **adjective** – characterized by or expressing a longing for the past

synonyms: homesick, sentimental, wistful

example: Every time I smell a wad of Play-Doh, **nostalgic** memories of my childhood come flooding back.

memory word: nah-stallion

picture: An old cowboy looking out the window of the retirement home is in a reverie as he watches the horses in a distant pasture. He *longs for the good old days* when he bred and raised stallions. A friend interrupts his daydream by asking, "You're thinking about that cute nurse, aren't you? You old dog." The cowboy responds *wistfully*, "*Nah. Stallion*s."

quixotic: (kwik-**sot**-ik) **adjective** – extravagantly chivalrous or romantic; not sensible about practical matters; idealistic and unrealistic

synonyms: foolish, impractical, impulsive, starry-eyed, utopian

origin: Miguel Cervantes wrote the classic novel *The Ingenious Gentleman Don Quixote of La Mancha* to poke fun at the chivalric literature of the 1500s. Don Quixote's addled brain was filled with tales of knights and damsels in distress. His make-believe world demonstrated that the "age of chivalry" was not the golden age depicted in the literature of the day.

example: Turning all F's into all A's in two weeks is a **quixotic** dream. It would be more practical to accomplish this goal in a quarter or semester.

memory word: quick-audit

picture: A modern Don Quixote, on a first date with a woman, proclaims his love to her and declares they are a match made in heaven. He *impulsively* proposes they quit their jobs and travel the world. First, he does a *quick audit* of his finances and discovers he has only $194.28 in his savings account. The *impractical fool* says, "That should do it, my love. The world is ours! Let's go pack our bags."

opaque: (oh-**payk**) **adjective** – too dark/thick for light to pass through

synonyms: cloudy, dense, dull, foggy, muddied, murky, obfuscated

origin: From the Latin *opacus*, meaning "shaded, darkened, obscure."

example: Superman can see through any **opaque** object, except lead.

memory word: OK

picture: The superhero SpectoMan attempts to help a boy develop X-ray vision so he too can see through *dense* objects. The kid tries so hard his head looks like it might explode. SpectoMan says, "*OK,* stop! Don't try so hard! You're going to have an aneurism or pop a hernia. Just relax and concentrate on that brick wall."

impervious: (im-**pur**-vee-uhs) **adjective** – not able to be penetrated, injured, or impaired; incapable of being influenced, persuaded, or affected

synonyms: immune, impenetrable, impermeable, invulnerable, resistant

origin: From the Latin *impervius*, meaning "cannot be passed through."

example: Lead is **impervious** to Superman's X-ray vision.

memory word: him-her-bs

picture: During a therapy session, a psychologist rolls his eyes because his patient is utterly incapable of telling the truth. Her psyche is *resistant* to the therapy, and her thinking is *impaired*. As she shovels *him her bs,* he wonders why he *can't penetrate* her thick skull.

lax: (laks) **adjective** – not strict or careful enough about work, rules, ideas, or standards of behavior; emptying easily or excessively

synonyms: careless, casual, derelict, flaccid, lenient, slipshod, sloppy

origin: From the Latin *laxus*, meaning "wide, loose, open."

example: Homer Simpson has a **lax** attitude about the safety precautions at the Springfield Nuclear Power Plant.

memory word: wax

picture: Your job at the *wax* museum is to monitor the thermostat and ensure a cool temperature. On your first day at the job, you are *careless and neglectful*, too busy with Facebook to notice that the air conditioner has stopped working. By the time you notice, the *wax* figures have melted.

apprehensive: (ap-ri-**hen**-siv) **adjective** – fearful about something that might happen

synonyms: anxious, disquieted, frightened, hesitant, nervous, worried

example: Lucy was **apprehensive** about leaving her home in Venezuela to immigrate to the United States. She worried that she wouldn't be able to learn English, but as it turned out, she is a quick study and mastered the language within a year.

memory word: apple-hen-sieve

picture: It rains apples and hens. An enormous sieve screens out the hens, but lets the apples fall into a boiling kettle of water below. The smaller hens are *fearful* they might fall through the *apple hen sieve*.

undulate: (**uhn**-juh-layt) **verb** – to move with a wavelike motion; to display a smooth rising and falling, or side-to-side alternation of movement

synonyms: oscillate, ripple, surge, swing, wave, wobble

origin: From the Latin *unda*, meaning "wave."

example: My heart and soul surge with patriotism when I see the Stars and Stripes **undulating** in the wind.

memory word: ninja-late

picture: Ninjas watching a martial arts match at a national meet have fun doing *"the wave."* The waves are almost perfect, but one ninja's timing is off. This ***ninja*** is ***late*** by a half second each time. I bet he could kick your butt, though!

forsake: (fawr-**sayk**) **verb** – to leave someone or something, especially when you have a responsibility to stay; to give up or renounce something you enjoy

synonyms: abandon, abdicate, desert, forswear, quit, renounce, repudiate

example: It would be selfish and irresponsible to **forsake** your family and job and retire to a Caribbean island.

memory word: four-snakes

picture: The doorbell rings and you open the door to find *four snakes* standing there with their luggage. They announce they are moving in, whether you like it or not. You run screaming into the street, *abandoning* the house and the rest of your belongings—for good.

turgid: (tur-jid) **adjective** – ostentatiously lofty in style; abnormally distended by fluid or gas

synonyms: bloated, bombastic, grandiloquent, pompous, pretentious

origin: From the Latin *turgidus*, meaning "swollen, inflated."

example: The author's **turgid** prose appeals to few young readers.

memory word: turgent (detergent)

picture: A woman allergic to just about everything washes her clothes in a detergent she found on sale, instead of her usual hypoallergenic detergent. Big mistake! Her body becomes covered in hives and her face and tongue are *swollen*. She finds herself in the emergency room being treated for an allergic reaction to the cheap detergent. The doctor asks her what happened and all she can say with a swollen tongue is, *"turgent."*

exonerate: (ig-**zon**-uh-rayt) **verb** – to clear as of an accusation; to free from guilt or blame

synonyms: absolve, acquit, exculpate, let off, pardon, release, vindicate

origin: From the Latin *exonerare*, meaning "to remove a burden."

example: The police recovered the store's security camera data, which **exonerated** the person accused of stealing the merchandise.

memory word: eggs-on-a-rake

picture: You and another guy clean the chicken pens every day. One evening, Colonel Sanders discovers hundreds of crushed eggs in the chicken pens. He inspects your rake; it is clean, so you are *free from blame*. However, upon inspection of the other guy's rake, the colonel finds it covered with smashed eggs. He says, *"Eggs on a rake is a smoking gun. Obviously, you can't be trusted. Grab your things and go!"*

rectitude: (rek-ti-tood) **noun** – rightness of principle and moral virtue

synonyms: honesty, integrity, morality, probity, righteousness

origin: From the Latin *rectus*, meaning "straight."

example: Every good boy does fine if he has moral **rectitude**.

memory word: wrecked-a-nude

picture: Driving home from church, a man of the cloth known for his *moral virtue and uprightness* spots a marquee for a nude dancing place advertising, "PREACHER NIGHT. NO COVER CHARGE. FREE DRINKS." Blind with rage, he loses control of the car and crashes into the front of the establishment. As usual, the media twists the facts into a sensational story to sell more papers. One headline reads, "Sinister Minister: Rectitude or *Wrecked a Nude*?"

quotidian: (kwoh-**tid**-ee-uhn) **adjective** – typical of what happens every day in the ordinary course of events

synonyms: commonplace, customary, daily, every day, mundane, routine

origin: From the Latin *quotidianus*, meaning "daily, every day."

example: Savannah's parents have told her a thousand times to complete her **quotidian** obligations—chores, homework, and piano practice—before watching TV.

memory word: quote-idiot

picture: A teacher's colleagues call him a *"quote idiot"* because he *routinely* misquotes well-known maxims, emphasizing his mistakes with air quotes. This morning, instead of saying "If you don't stand for something you will fall for anything," he got mixed up as *usual* and told his class, "If you fall for everything you don't stand for nothing."

surfeit: (**sur**-fit) **noun** – an overabundant supply; an uncomfortably full feeling due to excessive eating or drinking

synonyms: crapulence, glut, overindulgence, repletion, satiety, surplus

example: After Thanksgiving dinner, Troy rubbed his belly and moaned about the **surfeit** in his stomach, which was caused by a **surfeit** of turkey and dressing, cranberry sauce, mashed potatoes, gravy, yams, buttered rolls, and pumpkin pie.

memory word: surf-it

picture: A surfer dude lies on the beach, groaning and rubbing his belly. His buddy, carrying a surfboard, runs by and says, "Dude. The weather report said we can expect record waves today. You wanna find the perfect wave and *surf it?*" The first surfer responds, "You kidding me, dude? I just scarfed down a dozen fish tacos. I can barely move."

verdant: (vur-dnt) **adjective** – green with vegetation; covered with growing plants or grass; of the color green; inexperienced or unsophisticated

synonyms: flourishing, grassy, leafy, lush

origin: From the Latin *viridis*, meaning "green."

example: Mia is fascinated by the satellite photo of Earth, with its clear contrast of **verdant** and desert regions.

memory word: bird-ant

picture: A bird and ant play the game "Army." They camouflage themselves by attaching *green vegetation* to their uniforms. Their little *bird/ant* army, covered with *grass*, moss, and leaves, successfully blends in with the surrounding *greenery*.

trenchant: (**tren**-chuhnt) **adjective** – forceful and effective in expressing ideas; sharply perceptive

synonyms: articulate, biting, explicit, graphic; incisive, keen, penetrating

example: Harley found his professor's instructions for the research project **trenchant** and easy to follow.

memory word: trench-ant

picture: Ants serving as common laborers on a construction crew busily dig a trench. One *trench ant* is especially *articulate*. His *effective expression* convinces the others to work harder so he can lean on his shovel all day.

somnolent: (**som**-nuh-luhnt) **adjective** – tending to cause sleep; sleepy or drowsy

synonyms: asleep, dozy, listless, slumberous, snoozy, soporific

origin: From the Latin *somnus*, meaning "sleep."

example: Lunch always leaves Shayne in a **somnolent** state, often leading to a nap.

memory word: some-Nolan

picture: A salesman knocks on the door of an insomniac. When the man answers the door, yawning and rubbing his eyes, the salesman says, "Hi, my name is Nolan. I sell things that help you *sleep.* I've got Unisom, Sominex, valerian root, chamomile tea, and melatonin tablets." Mr. Exhausted barely lets him finish before groaning, "I'll take *some Nolan.*"

congenial: (kuhn-**jeen**-yuhl) **adjective** – having an agreeable, suitable, or pleasing nature

synonyms: affable, convivial, cordial, genial, harmonious, neighborly

example: Sheila and Tanja are **congenial** co-workers who like each other and enjoy carpooling to and from work.

memory word: fun-genie-owl

picture: You rub a lamp and a genie owl pops out. The *pleasant* owl puts its wing around you and promises a fun time. Every time you make a wish, the *fun genie owl* laughs and says, "Now, isn't that a hoot?"

inimical: (ih-**nim**-i-kuhl) **adjective** – unfriendly, harmful, or hostile

synonyms: adverse, hurtful, injurious, unfavorable

origin: From the Latin *inimicus*, meaning "unfriendly, an enemy."

example: Many members of the U.S. Congress are **inimical** to our constitutional liberties.

memory word: an-M-I-call

picture: An *unfriendly* M expresses his *hostility* by bullying kids on the playground. Now that's *an M I call* mean!

modicum: (**mod**-ih-kuhm) **noun** – a moderate or small amount, generally used to mean "any at all"

synonyms: iota, jot, little, shred, smidge, speck, tinge, trifle, whit

origin: From the Latin *modicus*, meaning "moderate, scanty, small."

example: Wacky Wanda, one of the top mobsters on Facebook's Mobsters, has not a **modicum** of sympathy for her victims.

memory word: Monica

picture: *Monica,* wearing her favorite dress, waits in line for school pictures with her friend Lily. Pointing out a stain on *Monica*'s dress, Lily reassures her, "Don't worry about that *little speck*. It's such a *small amount* that it's hardly noticeable."

adumbrate: (a-**duhm**-brayt) **verb** – to describe roughly or briefly or give the main points or summary of; to foreshadow

synonyms: indicate, outline, sketch; augur, bode, foretell

origin: From the Latin *adumbrare*, meaning "to represent something in outline."

example: Holden, the star of the Mustangs soccer team, **adumbrated** a game plan at halftime, turning the game around for a big Mustang win.

memory word: a-dumb-brain

picture: Jars of brains are lined up on a shelf in a mad scientist's lab. The ringleader has **outlined** the plan for their escape. *A dumb brain* says, "I know you done *give the main points* five or three times, but what I'm posed to do, again?" This doesn't *bode* well for a successful escape.

discursive: (dih-**skur**-siv) **adjective** – moving from topic to topic without order; reaching a conclusion by reasoning or argument rather than intuition

synonyms: deviating, digressive, erratic, meandering, rambling

origin: From the Latin *discursus*, meaning "running about."

example: The prosecutor delivered a **discursive** summation to the jury. Some jurors thought she made a lot of sense, presenting the evidence in an orderly way, but others couldn't keep track of her argument.

memory word: this-cursive

picture: Returning your graded essay, your literature teacher says, "*This cursive* penmanship is the best I've ever seen, but your essay is horrible. You *ramble* on about nothing. You *digress* from the topic sentence in the first paragraph and *wander* aimlessly toward the conclusion."

impinge: (im-**pinj**) **verb** – to make an impression; to have an effect or impact; to encroach

synonyms: infringe, intrude, invade, obtrude, violate

origin: From the Latin *impingere*, meaning "to drive into, strike against."

example: If the Founding Fathers were alive today, they would initiate another revolution upon discovering how much the ruling class has **impinged** on our constitutional rights.

memory word: him-pinch

picture: At a restaurant, you notice an old man who keeps pinching his waitress on the cheek and telling her she is the "cutest thing." He is *encroaching and infringing* on her personal space. The constant pinching is *making an impression* on her cheek; it is red and swollen. You've seen *him pinch* her at least a dozen times.

brusque: (bruhsk) **adjective** – abrupt to the point of rudeness

synonyms: blunt, curt, discourteous, gruff, impolite, short, snippy, terse

example: DMV employees are notorious for their inefficiency and **brusque** manner.

memory word: brush

picture: The haircutter points to the chair at her station and *curtly* orders, "Sit." Next, instead of nicely asking you how you want your hair cut, she *impolitely* demands, "What do you want?" If you move your head the slightest bit after she positions it the way she wants it, she *rudely* whacks you on the head with a *brush*.

tantamount: (tan-tuh-mount) **adjective** – equivalent in significance or value

synonyms: commensurate, equal, identical, like, same as, synonymous

example: These days, any criticism of the president is **tantamount** to racism.

memory word: tanned-amount

picture: Identical twins frequent a tanning salon. One uses the tanning bed and the other gets a spray-on tan. They emerge with *identical* tans. The cashier charges them the *same* amount for each tan. The *tanned amount* is *equivalent in value*.

zealous: (zel-uhs) **adjective** – enthusiastically devoted to something

synonyms: ardent, enthusiastic, fanatic, fervent, impassioned, passionate

example: I wrote this book because I am **zealous** in my dedication to help you build your vocabulary.

memory word: jail-bust

picture: A couple of convicts *enthusiastically* dig a tunnel to bust out of jail. They are *ardent* and *passionate* about this *jail bust*.

specious: (**spee**-shus) **adjective** – having deceptive attraction or allure; apparently but not really genuine or correct

synonyms: beguiling, deceptive, delusive, fallacious, misleading

origin: From the Latin *species*, meaning "appearance, surface."

example: Arriving at our campsite after dark, we saw the beautiful lake in the moonlight. However, the lake's beauty turned out to be **specious**. The next morning, we saw that it was polluted and devoid of life.

memory word: spaceship

picture: Your doorbell rings. When you open the door, you're surprised to see a *spaceship* in your front yard and several three-foot-tall aliens on your doorstep. The aliens shout, "Trick or Treat!" After you fill their bags with treats, they pick up their cardboard *spaceship* and proceed to the next house. They look so authentic—no wonder you were *misled!*

relegate: (**rel**-i-gayt) **verb** – to assign to a lower position, place, condition, class, or kind

synonyms: consign, demote, downgrade, pass on, refer

origin: From the Latin *relegare*, meaning "to remove, dismiss, send away, put aside."

example: Because the quarterback threw too many interceptions and incomplete passes, the coach **relegated** him to benchwarmer.

memory word: umbrella-gate

picture: Remember the Grimms' fairy tale of Hansel & Gretel and the wicked witch in the gingerbread house? Well, the witch just built a scrumptious gate for the fence surrounding her property. Unfortunately, the gate is made of sugar and will dissolve in the rain. On rainy days, you are *assigned to the lowly position* of holding a huge umbrella over the gate so it doesn't melt. Sucks to be the *umbrella gate* attendee!

benign: (bih-**nahyn**) **adjective** – showing kindness and gentleness

synonyms: benevolent, favorable, friendly, harmless, humane, innocuous

origin: From the Latin *benignus*, meaning "kindhearted, friendly."

example: Most of the time this word is used to describe a tumor; as in a **benign** tumor.

memory word: be-mine

picture: By all appearances, the ugly beast is mean, gruff, and harmful. In fact, he is *gentle, kind, and harmless*. He approaches a beautiful princess and presents her with a flower, saying, "Would you *be mine?*"

acclaim: (uh-**klaym**) **verb** – to acknowledge publicly the excellence of a person or act; **noun** – strong approval or praise

synonyms: approve, commend, praise; applause, commendation

origin: From the Latin *acclamare*, meaning "to cry out at."

example: Mark Twain is a highly **acclaimed** author.

memory word: a-clam

picture: *A clam* looks up at you from a plate. He *applauds, and praises* you for not eating him.

asylum: (uh-**sahy**-luhm) **noun** – an institution for the care of the mentally ill; an inviolable refuge or sanctuary

synonyms: haven, hideaway, retreat, safe house, shelter

origin: From the Latin *asylum*, meaning "sanctuary."

example: Refugees who escaped Cuba's brutal dictatorship were granted **asylum** if they made it to the U.S.

memory word: a-silo

picture: A businessman wants to leave the rat race and find *refuge* in a quiet *sanctuary*. He daydreams about renting space in *a silo* on a farm.

blithe: (blahyth) **adjective** – without thought or regard; joyous or merry in disposition

synonyms: carefree, cheerful, heedless, joyful, light-hearted, mirthful

example: There was a jolly miller once, lived on the river Dee. He worked and sang from morn till night, no lark more **blithe** than he.

memory word: scythe

picture: Whom do you know that is always happy and *worry-free?* Well, picture him or her in a field of tall grass. He or she is *whistling without a care in the world* while swinging a *scythe* and cutting the grass.

instigate: (in-sti-gayt) **verb** – to bring about, as by incitement or urging

synonyms: foment, incite, initiate, provoke, prompt, set off, stir up

origin: From the Latin *instigare*, meaning "to urge on, incite."

example: Interaction among delinquent peers seems to **instigate** crimes and escalate their severity.

memory word: against-the-gate

picture: Have you ever seen National Lampoon's *Vacation*? In this movie, the Griswold family drives cross-country to L.A. to vacation at Wally-World. They arrive to find it closed for repairs. This *provokes* Clark Griswold and *sets him off* into temporary insanity. Among other things, Clark punches Wally in the nose. Well, picture him or your dad at the entrance of Mellowstone National Park. A friendly bear stands at the closed gate explaining that a recent forest fire necessitates the temporary closure of the park. This *incites* Clark (or your dad) to shove him *against the gate* and start punching him in the nose, *provoking* the friendly bear to show his claws and teeth.

About the Author

Shayne Gardner is a former history teacher who constantly encouraged his students to develop a strong vocabulary. He put a new word on the whiteboard every day and quizzed the students every Friday. The students who turned the words into pictures, as instructed, aced the quizzes every week.

Shayne lives with his wife and daughter in Chandler, Arizona. He would prefer to reside in Hawaii, so please purchase several copies of this book and gift them to family and friends.

VisualizeYourVocabulary@gmail.com

VisualizeYourVocabulary.com

Facebook.com/VisualizeYourVocabulary

Pinterest.com/SATwerdnerd

Twitter.com/ SATwerdnerd

Google.com/+VisualizeYourVocabulary

Index

Index

Made in the USA
Middletown, DE
28 January 2017